LIVE

FROM THE

LONDON
PALLADIUM

LIVE

FROM THE

LONDON
PALLADIUM

NEIL SEAN

THE WORLD'S MOST FAMOUS THEATRE IN THE
WORDS OF STARS WHO HAVE PLAYED THERE

AMBERLEY

All pictures copyright of Maycon Productions
/ Pictures / Neil Sean Enterprises.

First published 2014

Amberley Publishing
The Hill, Stroud
Gloucestershire, GL5 4EP

www.amberley-books.com

British Library Cataloguing in Publication Data.
A catalogue record for this book is available from the British Library.

ISBN 978 1 4456 4313 7 (paperback)
ISBN 978 1 4456 4329 8 (ebook)

Typeset in 11pt on 12pt Sabon.
Typesetting and Origination by Amberley Publishing.
Printed in the UK.

Contents

The following book is dedicated to May and Con McCabe, Mr Philip Thompson, Mr Alan Scott, Mr Mark Grant and Ms Ann Montini, without whom the dream and the spotlights would have faded many curtain calls ago.

I would also like to thank the many cameraman, sound operators and happy snappers who have made all this possible: Edward Asta, Daniel Mason, Daniel Howard, Isidro Montero, Luca Roveri, Cris Mantio, Sharaz Ali and Juan Fernandez.

I was kindly assisted in this book by the wonderful Miss Jemma George. I wrote this book while staying at the Langham Hotel, London.

Follow me on Twitter at @neilsean1.

Introduction

The London Palladium has long held a fascination for me, as you will see from this book. The content is all taken from interviews with the stars, backstage staff and artistes who have appeared on the glorious stage of Argyll Street.

The content is not in any particular order, but rather in the way the interviews arrived. I know that I have only touched on a brief moment of many great stars' memories; the interviews have taken place in various locations, from TV studios in London, New York and Florida through to Yorkshire and even a boat in Norway. I hope you enjoy the stories about the stars who have performed in this variety house as much as I have enjoyed meeting them. Why not play 'Star Time', the theme from *Sunday Night at the London Palladium*, before you open another page? Transport yourself back to a time when stars were stars and Sunday nights meant staying in and seeing who was 'top of the bill' at the Palladium.

The Palladium Casts Its Spell

'It's every performer's dream to play the world famous London Palladium,' said my father, Alan Scott, himself a comedian. He married my mother Ann Montini, a variety artiste and theatre producer, and together they made sure I was raised on a rich diet of showbiz.

It was Dad's theory that you were no one in showbiz until you had walked on the hallowed stage of the London Palladium, home to the Royal Variety show ('the Show') – the biggest entertainment event on TV every year and a showcase for national treasures such as Tommy Trinder and Jewel & Warris, as well as for US legends including Judy Garland and Sammy Davis.

Coverage of the Show would start with the grand arrival of the Queen, greeted by celebrated producers – the impresarios – Louis Benjamin, Prince Littler and Bernard Delfont.

Our family would gather in the lounge, glued to our one TV – black and white in those days – waiting eagerly for the curtain to rise on this star-studded show. Unlike today, we had little idea who would appear on the stage. The BBC made it extra special back then; it was loaded with anticipation, free of advert breaks and provided a constant supply of talent, with bill-toppers such as Shirley McClaine and Julie Andrews and future stars like the Krankies, Roger De Courcey and Nookie Bear. All had truly earned their place on that stage.

It was another world to me – a wonderful world – but how nervous must these people have been, waiting for their moment to meet Her Majesty and appear in the Show? Not least the opening act – the comic who carried the weight of warming up the audience. This was, as Dad echoed throughout the evening, 'their make or break night'.

Despite my excitement and appreciation for the likes of Sir Norman Wisdom or the high-kicking Tiller Girls, I also felt strangely sorry for the acts. Regardless of how well they did, it seemed the audience – padded out in full dinner suits and diamonds – always looked to the royal box for guidance. If the royals laughed, they all laughed. The relief could take some of the shine from their moment of glory.

Even so, I vowed I too would one day walk that Palladium stage and was learning the craft of 'variety' entertainment early, thanks to mum and dad's own show, *Variety Express*.

Variety Express was what it said it was – variety and fast. The show enabled me to make my showbiz debut aged just seven, doing my best Larry Grayson at a theatre in Yorkshire. When I became older, the show developed even more and I am pleased to say we made a huge success of it, which included Tiller-style dancers, comics and singers who all got to play wonderful theatres like

Crewe Lyceum, Empire Consett and of course capital greats like the Hackney Empire and Arts Theatre in London. This really was my grounding in how to handle audiences and interact with them, but above all else, it was showbiz, pure and simple. The show was expertly produced by Ann Montini (Mum), while Dad handled the compère side of the show. It got great reviews, yet as my radio and TV career took off, plus Dad's blossoming solo shows and Mum's magazine work, we decided to call it a day in the early part of the millennium. A bigger factor, of course, was the theatre managers, who were clueless about PR, percentage deals and the basics of running a theatre. They were mystified by things like putting up a poster about the show prior to the performances rather than actually just popping one up while the show arrives. Little things, but vital to bums on seats, as we all know.

Route to the Palladium Greats

My personal and professional path has given me the opportunity to meet and interview many of the Palladium greats, who often confirmed my father's 'make or break' claim with comments like, 'You felt you had arrived,' and, 'Your career could start or indeed finish just by getting that one call to appear on the show.' The Royal Variety show at the Palladium was *the* golden ticket.

The showbiz legends within these pages may have waited years for such a prize – a prize that offered an extraordinary moment and true recognition of their talent, hard graft and ability to endure – names that we still know today. A very different 'prize', when we think of today's reality TV formats and seemingly instant fame, which often drops away just as fast.

That's me in the picture, standing centre stage at the Palladium. See dad, I told you I would do it and I'm happy to share the story.

Way back when, while trying to figure out how I would break into this world of showbiz, I struck lucky and was asked to appear briefly on a charity show at the theatre. I was unsure, until they said something magic: 'By the way, it's at the Palladium.'

I can't recall much about the event itself, but I was part of a giant sing-song towards the end of the show. Figuring I would get lost in the crowd and keen to capture the moment on film, I decided to have an afternoon rehearsal shot taken from the royal box (no less). If you look closely, you will see the fear in my eyes, but despite this fear I knew I would be back.

Here I am on stage for the first time at the London Palladium, rehearsing my bow to the Royal Box. It took me twenty years to return and they said it was a rebooking.

I have always worked hard for my professional goals – even in my work experience years (not always showbiz) – but I have also been so lucky to enjoy access to a glittering world of red carpets and press junkets. Some events are truly memorable, while others become a little familiar. With few exceptions, those staged at a theatre carry a spark of magic that is captured especially well on film. It seems the charm of old-fashioned theatres is very photogenic.

My first real job in the industry was to work as the entertainment reporter for Yorkshire television and then for Sky News, but it was a move to the major US network Fox News that gave me instant access to so many of the stars I had admired for so long.

I was asked by the station manager who I would most like to interview and he almost fell off his chair when I replied, without hesitation, 'Norman Wisdom.'

I guess my manager was expecting someone at the Oscars or Cannes as he questioned my choice. 'You want to interview Norman Wisdom – why?'

I explained that I was a huge fan of Wisdom's enduring work and that I was sure he would have some great stories. My father had worked with him at various events, so I was naturally enthusiastic about the idea and confident I would have the station manager's ear.

Alas, the manager crushed my world by saying, 'You can do that in your own time, we need real stars here on the channel,' and promptly told me to interview someone from a reality TV show whose name escapes me.

I felt the station manager was missing the point. I could be more vocal about my real thoughts towards him, but let's stick with 'missing the point'. Instead, I made efficient use of the TV studio and camera crew at my disposal. 'Downtime' was the best time, as it gave me the opportunity to build up some remarkable interviews with true showbiz legends.

It is a pleasure to now share these stories in their raw glory. Some may delight you, amuse you, or maybe even surprise you. To my own joy, they all allude to the magic of theatre and, in particular, 'appearing at the Palladium'. Not all of the stories are glamorous or finish with a happy ending. Some talk of fate, others of nerves or the challenge of both, but all are true – derived from the tapes that were never shown in full on TV.

I hope you enjoy the tales and I hope they reveal how the Palladium was such a life-changing experience for those lucky enough to appear on its stage.

Interviews with the Stars

Andrew Lloyd Webber
22 March 1948 – present

Andrew Lloyd Webber has created some of the most recognizable musicals of all time – from *Cats* to *Evita* to *The Phantom of the Opera*. He has collected a variety of honours, including a knighthood, seven Tony Awards, three Grammy Awards, an Academy Award and the Kennedy Center Honors Award. Songs from his musicals have gone on to experience wide popularity offstage as well and his theatre production company, the Really Useful Group, is one of the largest operating in London. He is, quite simply, a legend. While that word is overused, this is not the case with Lord Lloyd-Webber.

I have met Lord Lloyd-Webber on many occasions, including red carpet interviews and when he came to my studio to exclusively launch one of his musicals in Australia. He was as he always is: charming, polite and immune to praise about his outstanding work and music. As we sat in the stalls of his much-loved Palladium, we discussed why he bought it and what it meant to him.

Lord Lloyd-Webber had graciously agreed to an interview around the time of the launch of another of his successful musicals, *The Sound of Music*, which starred the newly created singer Connie Fisher, whom he would much rather talk about. As there always is when filming, a lull to reset the lights left us sat there looking towards the hustle and bustle of the stage, where, before our very eyes, a successful show was being created.

Lord Lloyd-Webber and I had first crossed paths years earlier when I auditioned for one of his shows, *By Jeeves*. I knew that I had no chance, but I loved the song 'Half a Moment' and figured if I got any chance to sing it on the West End stage then why not? But, like many of my auditions, while they loved the singing, 'The acting, oh dear, the acting!' I seem to remember the director wailing, as I walked off the stage to the sound of my own feet yet again.

Our next meeting was a tricky one, actually, because at that time Lord Webber had the huge film of his smash musical *Evita*, starring Madonna, about to go out to the world and the record production team of Mike Stock and Matt Aitken had done a cheeky cover of the hit song 'Don't Cry for me Argentina', which had a mix called 'Pre-Madonna mix'. Thankfully, he loved the disco version and all was saved once again, but I do recall the elegance of his Eton Square home and being made to feel welcome. So sitting here in the famous stalls left me pondering just what he we would talk about, and then he spoke.

'If you look at this wonderful Frank Matcham design, it never fails to take your breath away and I often sit here and look around, you know, take it all in. You're right, Neil, so many people have appeared in these hallowed walls and they all have earned their place on this stage, without a doubt.

'I could never sell the Palladium; for me it would have to be almost the end, you know, because I love it. It's a variety house in the best possible tradition and I think so many people have enjoyed hours upon hours of great entertainment here – I am glad that I will become a part of its history, I truly am.'

Like the professional that he is, it took a couple of takes for Lord Webber to get the 'tag line' right to conclude our TV interview – not because he was not good at it, but because we both ended up giggling, and then the usual happened and someone walked into shot just as the camera rolled. So finally we got the take and he thanked me for taking the time to come along and help promote his new show. While he thanked me, inside I was saying, 'No, honestly, no need,' but you try and conceal your nerves, don't you?

As long as we have Lord Lloyd-Webber, I know that the London Palladium is in very safe hands, and for that we should all be grateful.

Mr Gareth Parnell
Current London Palladium manager

Meeting Gareth is always a delight, as his enthusiasm and welcome is second to none, but I have a lot to thank Gareth for as he was the man who finally made my dream – to bring my one-man show to the theatre – come true and went above and beyond in helping me make it a sell-out success. We met to film a documentary with Gareth in the Val Parnell bar and it surprised me that Gareth is, in fact, a very shy man and not too happy being in front of the camera, but with gentle persuasion and like a true Palladium pro he gave us everything we needed to make it a success. I asked him if he had any ambitions to do anything else but manage the theatre, which he has now done for over twenty-five years to great success, but his answer surprised me.

'No – my ambitions lie here, really. If something came up, I'd look at it, but I have such an allegiance to this theatre in particular that it would be hard to tear myself away. I could go and do something else, but why would I? This is a calling, it's almost a vocation really, and I do feel like I'm the guardian of this theatre. If somebody tells me I have to go then I suppose I have to go, but until then I am going nowhere,' he said, laughing.

Gareth added, 'I think everyone has a story about the theatre and you know, so much has happened here, but it's a great place to work. We have a tight team and of course I can call on the expertise of Linford, but yes, for me this is it – I may even be carried out of her!'

I asked Gareth if he has witnessed any disasters since

been the manager and, polite as ever, he smiled and said that there had been a few, but that there was one that sticks out in his mind. 'The one that haunts is when we had Prince Charles and Camilla come to see a performance of *Chitty Chitty Bang Bang*, and the first thing that happened was that there were two sets of tickets for their seats, and the other party arrived first and refused to get out of their seats – they were double-booked. I know, can you imagine? And I have them stood at the back of the theatre being ever so nice, and waiting and waiting, but I was going a slightly different colour.

'A rather shadowy man in a dark suit came over to me and said, "You will do whatever it takes to get His Royal Highness in his seats, or else." So I offered this other party two bottles of champagne and I think almost everything I owned to get them to switch seats and they kept me sweating and waiting, you know, the full drama.

'They were a very fun couple who I think enjoyed seeing me turning puce with fear. He was from Ireland and a journalist, so he is also seeing a good story here, and I'm thinking, "Oh no, will this be splashed all over the press now?" and he said to me, "Who are these seats for, if you don't mind me asking?"

'So I said, "The Prince of Wales and Camilla Parker Bowles," and he kept me hanging on for a little while longer before he actually agreed to leave the seats. Thankfully, the prince had no idea, but then on the same night the set broke down and the show had to be axed at half time, so yeah, that is one I remember the most! It's not that you forget that kind of thing, is it?'

As Gareth has met almost every major star over the last twenty-five years, I wondered if he ever got star-struck himself and he told me, 'Only meeting you, Neil! No, truthfully, actually I've met pretty much anybody, from Michael Jackson to Madonna through to all the major royals, and it's wonderful and so exciting. But I think I must have a star-struck immunity gene. You just have to get on with it. It's not good to be star-struck, really, or you'd end up backstage every five minutes; of course I think it's not a good idea to have the manager looking like a wet dish cloth when he is in charge, now is it?' he laughed.

Gareth tells me that he is looking forward to reading this book. 'I would love to know so many of the stories of the big stars you have talked about in your show and I think the footage and archive must be amazing. But yes, anything that promotes my wonderful London Palladium has to be a good thing.'

Lena Zavaroni
4 November 1963 – 1 October 1999

One of the biggest influences I had at that time is one of my favourite Palladium greats, the singer Lena Zavoroni.

She was discovered on the famous TV talent show *Opportunity Knocks*, which was hosted by Hughie Green, and was a superstar from the word go. She had it all – great personality, good looks and a voice that defied her years; plus she really was talented. This girl, who I met briefly a few times thanks to our paths crossing at summer seasons in glamorous resorts like Bridlington and Great Yarmouth, was such a nice lady.

I recall being in awe of her at Bridlington when she was starring in the summer season at the Spa Theatre and really was holding the whole show together. I have to say that I felt as though the team around her then were less than friendly; as a kid you pick up on this quite quickly.

One incident I recall well was when we were all invited onto the beach to help promote the show and the resort. We had a collection of t-shirts with a banner on them claiming, 'I'm a Brid Kid.' It was a fun event, but while Lena wanted to join our group to chat and have fun she was quickly whipped away by an odd woman who was her manager, totally lacking in any charm or warmth. I remember thinking how lonely she must be, stuck with her all the time.

After Lena had hosted her own show at the Palladium we met up again at various functions and she was always kind and thoughtful. She had appeared in a Royal Variety show by then and had me stunned at her quick change act, right there on stage in front of the royals.

I remember asking her every detail of the show and she told me, 'It's all so fast and furious, but yeah, great fun. The week at the Palladium was manic but then again just great, because I'm starring in my own show there, can you believe it?'

I asked her if she needed any help and she kindly told me this, which I have never quite forgotten, 'Look, if you're down in London I can get the people to show us both around the Palladium and who knows? You may end up on the stage.'

Lena, I now know, was a bit older than me, but even during her darkest days she gave me kindness and hope. It's often said that great talent is never forgotten but in the case of her, sadly that is not the case. So, out of all the stars I have met, seen and loved at the Palladium, let's all spare a moment to remember the great young talent that was Lena Zavaroni.

Frankie Vaughan CBE
3 February 1928 – 17 September 1999

Frankie Vaughan was a true entertainment legend with a memorable crooner voice. He released more than eighty singles in his lifetime. He was known as 'Mr Moonlight', after one of his early hits, and fondly remembered for his stage props of a top hat and cane.

I was working a winter season at a hotel in Plymouth – a glorious area with stunning coastline and, of course, great people, but not the land of showbiz for a budding thespian, or so I thought.

I had no idea that Frankie Vaughan had checked into the hotel until I got a call from the restaurant manager, who informed me that 'we have a guest who wants to see you'. Alas, the request was not from him. Instead, a rather elegant lady with a hint of a Yorkshire accent explained that her husband – an entertainer – had returned hungry from a late night show but the restaurant had finished serving breakfast. Could I do anything to help?

I knew the chef was less than friendly and I paused to ponder the dilemma but said I would try my best. In a blink of an eye I was face to face with one of the greatest British entertainers of all time, Frankie Vaughan. I sensed he was about to elaborate on the complaint, but I simply stood back in awe and said, 'Mr Moonlight, it's really you.' He beamed a smile and said he was stunned that anyone my age would know who he was.

This was the man who had kissed and danced with Marilyn Monroe in his only Hollywood film, *Let's Make Love*. This was the man who charmed us all with his top hat and cane, singing 'Give Me the Moonlight' to swooning audiences in all the top variety theatres. Of course I knew who he was and he seemed delighted, albeit still in need of some breakfast.

I organised this swiftly and he asked me to join them while he spoke about his career and how he owed it all to an artiste called Hetty King. 'She told me the importance of dressing smartly, and more so, correctly, for any occasion,' he said, and it was clear that Miss King's words stood fast for well over fifty years. Frankie and his charming wife Stella looked immaculate, even at such an early hour.

Over coffee and toast, Frankie spoke more about his career and how and where he got discovered. He revealed, 'I also have Yorkshire to thank for many things – meeting my wife, Stella, who is my rock, and of course appearing at the City Varieties in Leeds where I first got noticed.'

Frankie had an easygoing way about him and was happy to share how he went on to top the bill at every major theatre in the UK and then became the first British singer to star in Las Vegas. He broke house records in cabaret at New York's Copacabana. 'I never thought in a million years that I would ever go down well in the US but they seemed to like my style and wit. Plus, of course, I was told I was not bad-looking then, so maybe that helped too,' he laughed.

Vaughan landed two number one hits, 'Tower Of Strength' and 'Garden Of Eden'. Perhaps more achievable was his ability to retain a strong and loyal fan base (of women of a certain age) through the pop and rock explosion of the sixties, despite punctuating his songs with high kicks and keeping those hat and cane props close at hand.

'People told me that the gimmick of the kick and the cane would not work,' he said, 'but I had other ideas, so I kept them in the act. They were my trademark and I think that is what I will be remembered for.'

Turning his attention to appearing at the most famous venue in the world, Frankie sighed. 'Ah, the Palladium. Well, let me tell you, Neil, the theatre has a great vibe about it. I don't mean this in a strange way, but it looks after its performers, and you know – you feel happy just being on that stage.' He went on to explain that he owed the Palladium a huge favour after recording his own show, *Star Time*, live from the theatre in 1959.

'We featured all my hits up to that point and the recording then became my very first album, which shot to the top of the charts – a million sellers – so yes, it holds a warm feeling for me, and you know, sometimes I just like to walk past the theatre. Don't ask me why, but I do. It's like saying thank you to the place for making so many of my dreams come true.'

Mike Winters
15 November 1930 – 24 August 2013

Mike Winters, born Michael Weinstein on 15 November 1930, and Bernie Winters, born Bernie Weinstein 6

September 1932, were English brothers and a very funny comedy double act.

I loved how they interacted and truly enjoyed their style of comedy. Mike, always dapper and in control, reeking of showbiz, was a real inspiration; Bernie was dimwitted to such great effect and a splendid foil to Mike. They were great siblings and an ideal partnership.

Mike and Bernie Winters enjoyed considerable and enduring success through theatre and panto seasons. It was the era of *Morecambe and Wise*, in the sixties and seventies – their greatest rivals and a hard act to follow – but they were sufficiently different and special to stand their own ground. For a while both acts were signed to the same agent and TV channel, ATV.

I first met Mike and Bernie in the seventies. They were appearing at the North Pier in Blackpool; at the time I had no idea it was to be their last big show together, but I read it later in a theatre newspaper. My father made the introduction – I felt very lucky and strangely 'large', not for the privilege but because so many of these TV legends appeared to be quite little, yet they carried sparkling good looks and oozed boyish charm.

I chatted briefly to Mike and Bernie on the pier, before they went into the theatre. I took a Polaroid snap – instant joy, yet sadly shortlived as the image has faded through time. My memory of the meeting, however, is still vivid and I could easily recall the tale as I prepared to meet Mike years later.

I, by this time, was working in TV full time and developing my own chat show, *Be My Guest*. Still running now, the show is unique in that it is syndicated around the world via various platforms; the best thing about the show is that the hos pick the guests. Because of that, I was able and am able to pick people that I know the public love and miss but who young TV bosses think are old hat.

We met again on what was to be Mike's last big TV interview – as a superstar guest on *Be My Guest*. He was joining me to talk about his book, *The Sunny Side of Winters*, described as light-hearted memoirs with some great stories through the years. This was a precious moment for me – I was excited yet nervous.

As we sat down in the studio, Mike looked at the crew and leaned towards me. He asked if I had read the book – of course – and told me, 'I have done so many interviews with young people like you and to be honest, they don't really know the business, which is hard on an old boy like me as I have to start again and explain why I am famous.' He chuckled at his comment and we all relaxed.

I had asked the reception staff, production crew and Felix our security man to say hello to Mike when he arrived. I explained to them that Mike was a huge star back in the day and we needed to respect that with polite acknowledgement and a smile. Everyone agreed – many of them in their twenties with no idea about the Winters – and was happy to play respectfully along. Perhaps this helped.

Mike began to regale us in the studio with his intriguing tales of a showbiz life. Young or old, we were fascinated with his every word.

I asked Mike just how he began his career and he explained in great detail that it was not an easy ride.

'We really started out as an act because I was getting nowhere as a musician. I loved playing the clarinet and all that but, truthfully, bookings were thin and while Bernie and I enjoyed being in the world of showbiz, it was not – let me tell you – making us rich.

'We used to do cabaret at the Cumberland Hotel in Marble Arch and kid ourselves that we were 'Up West' – you know, the big time. But the truth was we hardly ever got paid and when we did it was not great money, just enough to survive, really.

'It was Jack Good who really gave us the break.'

Jack Good was no ordinary producer. He was considered a pioneer of TV production and king of rock and pop artistry. He booked the Winters on the BBC's music and entertainment show, *Six Five Special* – a precurser to the format we now know as *Top of the Pops*. Their job was to fill in between the music and comedy acts. 'Yeah, right,' said Mike. 'But actually we did well, and then we could spend a little money on our act, or rather, our look.'

Mike explained that until then they both had basic suits – no evening dress, which was worn by most in the variety theatres. 'We needed to smarten up and show people that we were serious about the business. Once we had the suits, we had the attention of the much feared Cissie Williams. She was feared – yes, without a doubt. She was, if you like, a Simon Cowell character in her office, without the camera and the other panelists,' he laughed.

Cissie Williams was the main booker for the Moss Empire circuit, which included the London Palladium. She was the gate keeper for acts wanting 'in' on the big time and especially selective when it came to comedians for top variety bills. She felt too many comics on one show would confuse the audience.

From her office in Cranbourne Mansion in central London, Cissie could really make or break a career and often did so without shame. Strangely, only a few women seemed to stand up to Cissie. As comedian Hylda Baker explained, 'I was not frightened of her at all, oh no. She loved the men on the circuit, of course, because they fawned over her and made a fuss with flowers and stuff, whereas we women – what could we do? Oh yes, a formidable lady, but I also knew she was quite shy outside the job. I was lucky as I presented my own show and as such could do what I liked, even though she did not like it.'

Cissie enjoyed power and flattery but she had a particular thing about appearance. Good suits and clean shiny shoes were vital. Shopping for new suits straight after *Six Five Special* was a purchase into Cissie's world and on to the Moss Empire circuit. Mike explained, 'We were young, not bad-looking and she liked the idea that she could make you a star. I am sure she enjoyed that part of the process.

'We had been booked to play the Finsbury Park Empire, which was a great date for us, and Cissie was watching. Our shoes shone like beacons – they looked good. We did the act and all that, but Cissie showed little emotion – a laugh, I think, or maybe a smile – yeah, just a smile. At the end, she walked to the front of the stage, looked up at Bernie and me and calmly said, "I'll be in touch."

'We heard back later that she was not a fan of the

act at all – it left her puzzled – but she liked our shiny shoes and good suits. So we had a crap act but looked good, and to her, it was a start.' Those suits were a great investment.

So when did the Winters get to the Mecca of all the Moss Empires, the London Palladium?

Mike explained, 'I know everyone says this, but even for us, at that time, it was the place where we wanted to appear. I had seen all the huge American stars on the stage and figured that we as British should be up there too.

'I had many favourites from the London Palladium. Danny Kaye, who was simply brilliant, yet really when you broke it down did not have an act, as such; he was simply Danny Kaye. Others that struck me for star power were the likes of Judy Garland, oh, and Sid Field, who I just adored – I mean, the guy was a genius when you look back at it today. We laughed so much and we so wanted to be just like him. We both loved Albert Modely, "Our Albert" – another great comedian and yet, you know, quite a simple effect he had on the audience, because he was one of them and that was the key to it all really.

'Playing the Palladium was our goal and dream and, thanks to that Finsbury Park booking and Cissie, we were on our way. All the time, though, we were upping our look – everywhere we went people asked us to look smarter, just like "that nice Frankie Vaughn". Frankie was a huge star and we appeared with him many times. It was Hetty King who told him how to dress and look on stage, from the high kick to the cane. He shared his secrets of looking good, but as he had an expensive tailor we bypassed that part of the look,' laughed Mike.

Mike continued to muse over just why appearing at the Palladium had been so important to him and Bernie. 'It's a case of knowing that you have made it, you know – sat or stood on that stage where all the greats have appeared and more so, your peers – but my biggest memory is, of course, appearing there at the Royal Variety show in front of our dear Queen. She really is lovely, and so brave to sit through such a show when I am sure she would rather be at home feeding the corgis.

'That was our biggest break – the Palladium year. Bob Hope was top of the bill but we were seen as the great British hope for comedy that year, along with Cliff (Richard) and the Shadows; I figured we would clean up in the applause stakes. Even Bob Hope told us that he was worried just how well he would go down that night.

'Anyhow, in the afternoon we had a small run-through in the theatre. This was really just for the press, so that they could get it out who they thought was going to do well that night in front of the Queen.

'So we are doing well, laughs are aplenty and the press are lapping it up so much so that we are told that we are down to be the big hit of the show – that is, until the producer, Robert Nesbitt, comes backstage to see us and very brutally explains how we can't use certain elements of the act. When I say elements, I mean almost all of the act, and this is the Palladium – people are now expecting us to do well, yet all the jokes that Robert found too risqué are been cut.

'I would like to say at this point that they were tame by today's standards and all that, but it was the early sixties and people were far more worried about things like that back then. The upshot is that we now have no act and we have to devise one, pronto, so basically we went back to the old act from the fifties of me with the clarinet and Bernie mucking about. Not the best material, but you know, we're still on the show and the producer is happy even if we are not.

'So I'm not noticing that Bernie is getting more and more nervous as the show goes on, and backstage at the Palladium there is something of a party atmosphere, more so with the acts that have already been on and are now holding court and having a drink. People like Harry Secombe and Andy Stewart, who had a never ending flow of whisky, of which Bernie is now partaking to calm his nerves.

'We get on do the act and it goes okay, not great but just okay. Plus, our parents are there and my dad is thrilled. He comes backstage to meet people and is never in awe of the great stars, he is just looking at us as if he can't quite believe it – his two boys playing the Palladium and doing great. It was an emotional night. But more was to come. After the show you have the official line-up of acts to be presented to the Queen and her party and we are chosen to go into the line-up. I have to say, at this point I have noticed just how much swaying Bernie is now doing but I think it's okay, because what can go wrong now? After all, we have done the show and all is well – right?

'Wrong. We see the small door open at the side of the stage and up pops her Royal Highness and she looks very regal and beautiful and you know, we are in awe, really star-struck. I would say that, whatever anyone says, in those moments you are just dumbstruck because you are coming face to face with someone you would have never ever dreamed that you would meet.

'So she is talking to Cliff and the Shadows and then Norman Vaughn, who was the compère of the show, and near us is the great singer and sex symbol Eartha Kitt – I am now rigid with nerves and Bernie is swaying more than ever. The show's organiser Bernard Delfont introduces us and says, "Ma'am, this is Mike and Bernie Winters." I smile and offer my hand as we have been told to do; she offers hers and then there is a polite conversation.

'Then she offers her hand to Bernie, and he smiles and does his famous "Ehh …" smile with the teeth and says, "Alright Mum." No one says anything. She smiles but looks for help; she now thinks that she is trapped with a madman. I can't say anything at this stage as I am struck with fear of what could happen next. So Bernie, who is, shall we say, well lubricated, points to a panto poster at the side of the stage and says, "You fancy coming to see us in panto?" She smiles and he carries on, "I am serious, honest – bring the kids, I can get you tickets if you like, just let me know." She looks at Bernie Delfont, as if to say "get me out of here", so he finishes with, "Excuse me, Mum, but do you like Football? If not, can I have your tickets for the Cup Final? I'll report back the results and all that, but yeah, shame to waste them really, don't you think?"'

Mike laughs so much recalling this story that we have a break on camera as he has to recover to carry on, but carry on he does. 'I was not mad with Bernie, as you couldn't be really; in fact I think she quite enjoyed it, but the fun part was that no one told him off. So yeah, that is my biggest memory of the Palladium for us – the pinnacle really – and then, yes, we did the panto there with Frankie Vaughn, Joan Reagan, Jimmy Edwards, Dick Emery and Gillian Lynne, and we used to go to a great coffee shop near the theatre. That is the other thing that has changed, we all went out around the theatre together. Now it's all dark glasses, agents and managers, but back then in the Palladium we were just grateful to be actually working.

'The Palladium was good for us. I mean, we appeared on big shows there and *Sunday Night at the London Palladium*, which was live, you know. I mean, it was hair-raising looking back, but all good experience and the atmosphere on show day was electric really; but as I say, we were young and very keen to learn and work. We were at the Palladium, we were getting paid and we were doing something that we really enjoyed. We were in showbiz and in the showbiz Mecca of the world – the Palladium – so yes, we were very happy kids.'

As we leave the studio, Mike is on a high and tells me that he has really enjoyed reliving his Palladium days. I ask him who made the most impression on him from the theatre and, quick as a flash, he says, 'Jewell and Warris. They were great and were really the first comics that spoke to the audience. I saw them do their act at the Palladium and thought if only we could be as good as them, then, you know, we would have made it. So yeah, that would be the people that mattered to us both, as I know Bernie liked them too.'

Mike's final revelation: 'I often go back (to the Palladium) when I am in town you know, and just stand back and look at the old place. It still sends a shiver down my spine each time I see it and, for me, it was the greatest period of our professional careers in that theatre.'

Alan Scott (comedian)

As Alan took to the stage, he knew they were going to be a tough crowd. Why? Well, 600 screaming kids on a wet Saturday afternoon in November really did not care about seeing two young rising comics doing their best to take off the master Jimmy James. Who was Jimmy James to them? All they wanted to see was the Western and then receive some free sweets from Don Haigh, the kindly general manager of the Palace cinema in Heckmondwike.

As ever in the world of showbiz, the comedians were not being paid much but it was a show and money was money, so they battled on.

Alan Scott started his career when he was just fourteen years old, setting up his own touring variety-concert party and taking it to any theatre that would have him.

He tells me, 'When I started, the great days were coming to an end. I appeared at the Huddersfield Palace (soon to be student flats), but the theatres were desperate to keep hold of anything they could.'

Although it was called 'the Palace', by this time the Huddersfield was in dire need of renovation. It was masquerading under a new name, Le Continental, a move that angered many as tables had been added and food was now being served in the stalls while the acts were on. Things were changing, but not for the better.

Alan recalls, 'The late great Hylda Baker was appearing the week before our run. While this was a big time for us, even at her peak, Hylda could not command a full house. She actually lived in a caravan just opposite the theatre and yes, she had the famous Monkeys with her. A lovely lady, who offered us support when we came to check out the theatre the week before. We didn't really need to "check it out" – I lived nearby and was a regular – that was me just trying to act as if I knew what I was doing, to be honest,' he admitted, laughing.

'After our week there the manager took me to the bar and suggested that, as he was moving on, I should apply for the job of assistant manager of running the theatre. "You're young, got good ideas and know what this lot (the audience) want, so why not give it a crack?" The theatre at this time was managed by the McNaughton group, who had offices in London, so it seemed a world away from the one we all lived in. Our week at the Palace was a great success due mainly to the fact we were local and because I did most of my own PR, which was vital, looking back. The week after, they had a nude show in and suggested that we come back to "help out"; the thing is, my mum flatly said no. After all I was just past sixteen and, well, this was racy stuff.

'The following week we were at the Keighley Hippodrome, which of course has often been cited for breaking the great Shirley Bassey; by the time we were playing it, like in so many theatres, up and coming acts were dying and they were using any methods they could to bring in the audience. At the Hippodrome, we decided to formulate an idea that some could say was a precursor to the talent shows of today. *Top Town* was basically a talent show with the next town over, bringing in double the audience – it was a great success and filled the theatre twice nightly with a great spend at the bar. Looking back, the prizes also were nothing like they are today. I mean, I think it was a fish and chip supper along with a haircut. Can you imagine doing that today and actually getting away with it?'

Alan recalled the days of appearing at the Middleborough Empire with Jimmy Young. He was seen as a pop star back then and as almost corrupting the morals of youth with his rock 'n' roll songs. Alan added, 'I was lucky enough to meet and work with many of my idols, including the wonderful Frank Randle, Al Reed and so many other big names, thanks to my quest to appear in the Mecca of showbiz back in the fifties – Blackpool. Frank was indeed a gentleman and was nothing like the character he appeared to be on screen or on stage. Al Reed was, as has been reported many times, something else, really. He enjoyed the finer things in life and it showed, but I do think that went against him in the end as the people who adored him were in fact working class and so in reality he should have stayed with them. Great comic, though; perfect timing and something of a hero of mine.'

Alan has fond memories of working in variety at the famed resorts of England, in particular Hornsea, on the east coast of Yorkshire. 'It was a big event, to get that season for me; I had never done one before and to see my name in huge billboards over the Star Cinema was a joy. The manager was, of course, wonderful at PR and loved knowing that we had a summer show. Our rival was a summer follies at the Floral Hall and I am thrilled to say we beat them at the box office.' Alan adds, 'Going to a resort in those days was in fact a big event. You had made it if you could get so many weeks during the summer. I was so excited and nervous at the same time, but the weeks went by quickly. In those days the mark of a successful show, of course, was the patronage of the mayor. He attended our show and basically gave it the thumbs up in the town, which saw the masses of nearby Scarborough, Withernsea and the like all coming to see the show.

'The show consisted of a basic cine variety programme, in which I, as the compère and comedian, had to hold it all together, but the fun night was Friday, when we hosted the local "Miss Hornsea" competition. It was a huge event covered by the media, including TV and Radio. Girls from all over the regions came over to take part in the event – those beauty contests were the life blood of the sea side holiday trade. We had a ball with it and, of course, the locals came out in force. The judges changed weekly and basically it was who was available and who was in town; Alex Munro was a great judge and got into the spirit no end. It was all so innocent then, of course – our other big show stopper was a real corker; "Tape a Tune", which is in the title – people, can you imagine, taped a tune into a recorder that they had "played themselves". Guess what? We had judges, just like *X Factor* and *Britain's Got Talent* have today, and they would decide who had won and what. The show went down a storm and the winner got a brand new state-of-the-art tape recorder to "Tape a Tune".

'During the season we also had visits from major film stars whose films were showing during the day. One was a real comedy legend by the name of Norman Wisdom. He was super and stayed for the show, so for me, appearing with such a comic genius on stage in his first summer season was beyond the realms of what showbiz was all about! David Whitfield also popped by, being a local Hull lad, and many others, too, who all came along to plug their movies. Many of the leading actresses of the day also brought along their own flowers, which were to be presented to them on stage by me after the film. They had to, as even then, budgets for promotion were tight.

'As the summer came to a close and the whole team reflected on the success of the show, I was over the moon to receive offers. Jack Taylor, a huge respected producer in the Blackpool scene, had written with an offer; Star Cinemas also offered me the chance to run my own cinema with variety included – thrilling stuff for a kid from Yorkshire. Butlins, Pontins, they all heard that this was the summer show to be seen. Did I take the offers on board? Well, what I did do was sign up to run the variety shows at the New Theatre, Huddersfield, for the famed and much feared impresario Ms Nita Valerie. I enjoyed that too, but then the call came for the world famous Palladium and, of course, while this was a one-off special show for the services and on a Sunday, when I could take the day off, I jumped at the chance, basically.

'You see, landing that tiny spot on a show that was booked in for one night was the making of me, really,' Alan revealed. 'I was lucky enough not to have got stuck there by doing a big show and, while I loved it and the experience, I had also already appeared at big theatres like Hackney Empire, Finsbury Park and so forth. But yes, the Palladium I knew would help me career-wise. I think, looking back, we did not know just how lucky we were then to work in such fine times with regards to the world of showbiz. Mr Val Parnell was the boss of the theatre and everyone knew it; in a way, that was a good thing, because you know, there was none of this casual chat or over-friendliness with him. You were booked and there to make money and draw the crowds in. Well not me, as such, but the top of the bill. I do recall him not being as friendly to others and so forth, yet he was what a manager should be, stylish and in command. Playing the Palladium, as I am sure you will find out, Neil, adds something to your prestige as a performer and while others may laugh and say, "Oh well, it was only once on a lowly charity night," at least you can say you walked on that stage and appeared on the same spotlight as the greats, like Max Miller, Joe Church and so on.' Alan also recalled that not all performers actually liked the call to appear at the Royal Variety when at the Palladium, for one simple reason – money. "Oh yes, it was a great call and all that but back then the show was not televised as it is now and, in a way, that was also a blessing, as not many people saw your act. It was not dissected and talked about; it was more like an exclusive club that saw you. Then the friends and enemies who read about you in *The Stage* or *The Performer* knew you had appeared there. But many acts hated the call as they had to cover all the costs themselves and this could run into quite a lot of money.'

Alan carried on, 'The suit, band parts and then new material, which all had to be passed by the producer, all came out of your pocket and that did not appeal to all the entertainers that were offered the slot. I recall chatting to Max (Miller), who always liked to go on first at any theatre so that he could get the last train back to Brighton, and he would say how much he was not a fan of it because of the money and, of course, to him it would have meant staying around in the smoke for another night as he missed the late train back.'

Alan returned to the Palladium a few years back and had a tour of the place; he was also asked to entertain with one of his 'Audience with ... ' style shows to former workers and fans of the place. He told me, 'It's funny, really. When you're young, you're nervous and think the theatre is huge and a massive problem to fill and perform in, yet now I can see with experience it does not go that far back. While it was daunting to a nineteen-year-old boy, at this age you simply would just take all that in your stride and hope that the Palladium and the laughs would just help you through.' Watching Alan entertain the crowds at the show, this time in one of the bar areas, it really was like having a masterclass in how to handle an audience. As I left the bar area where he was entertaining, amid the howls of laughter and 'oh dear's at yet another joke of his, he winked, and I got the feeling that he and the Palladium would be just fine.

Jason Donovan
1 June 1968 – present

Australian actor, singer, stage performer, reality show celebrity and TV presenter, Jason Donovan was born on 1 June 1968 and is well known to many more of 'today's' generation. I have been lucky enough to interview and spend time with Jason Donovan on many occasions, firstly while working with him on his hit recording career and now when he comes along to the studio to promote his latest album or show, or simply as a great chat show guest.

Jason shot to fame playing the lovable rogue that was Scott Robinson in *Neighbours*, which really was the must-watch soap of the late eighties.

He told me, 'We were filming back in Oz. We had no idea how big the show had become here in the UK, so when I finally arrived to do some promo I clicked on to how fast this was all taking off. Then, thanks to Kylie's pop star success with Stock Aitken Waterman, they offered me a similar deal.'

Jason had reservations, though. He said, 'Looking back now – Stock Aitken Waterman were genius in crafting hit after hit for so many people time after time. I was so young and immature. I really wanted to become a rock star and not a pop star, but the opportunity was there.

'I recorded my first single with them, "Nothing Can Divide Us", which, by the way, had been turned down by Rick Astley. I had no idea how the lyrics suited the situation I was in with my then girlfriend Kylie.

He added, 'Looking back and being older, of course, I can now see how it appealed to the masses. Hindsight is a great thing, is it not?'

Jason Donovan went onto to sell over 3 million albums and was the most talked about and biggest selling artiste of 1989, a feat that still sees him shocked and reflective. 'When you're young you think this will last forever and ever but, of course, pop is littered with these people, and I know from my career that it can have its ups and downs.' Indeed, by the early 1990s Jason was slipping away from his pop public, and fast. The audience was moving away from the Stock Aitken Waterman sound and prospective hits were struggling to make the top notch.

Fortunately for Jason, he was approached for a role in a musical and, he explained, 'It was something that came out of the blue, really. I mean, I knew of Lord Webber, of course – the man is a musical genius – but I did think, is this right for my career? How would it be perceived by my fans and future fans, if there were any at all?

'I was told the musical was "Joseph" and I was a fan, but truthfully, Neil, the seal on the deal was that it would be at the Palladium. I know people say that but I spoke to my father Terry, who is also an actor, and he was over the moon about the deal and I agreed it there and then. I had limited stage experience and, thinking back, I must have had masses of confidence to think I could fill that huge stage; but it appears that I could, and they hoped my fan base would come with me.'

Jason, as ever, is modest, because it was in fact Lord Webber's beautiful daughter Imogen who was the brains behind this idea. She had heard that her father was keen to revisit the hit musical and she made the suggestion that Jason – the blond pop god – would be just the ticket for young girls like her who would love to see him in such an epic production. So, after a careful chat with dad, the idea was put into play.

Mike Stock, the writer and producer of all of Jason's big hits, told me that at the time there was even talk about the famous trio – Stock, Aitken and Waterman – hooking up with Lord Webber to create and add a new song to the show, which, he admits, 'Sadly never happened, but I think it's a shame, in a way, because we were at the height of our game and, combined, we could have made a huge hit with a new song.'

Whatever the reasons behind the song that never was, the most famous track from the show – 'Any Dream Will Do' – was quickly recorded with Nigel Wright and a video was filmed and released with the single. It shot to the top of the charts and put Jason in good stead for a long run at the Palladium. It worked, too, as the box office advance was going through the roof and the show was already a sell-out for months prior to opening. Jason remembers this with pride. 'I was so happy, not because of me but because of the faith that people had put in me. When Lord Webber turned up, he would be happy, knowing that whatever the critics said about me we would have a successful show.'

Jason tells me that walking into the theatre for the first time is something he will never forget. 'I do think it's something all performers go through there, really. I mean, everyone who walked through that stage door – well, it's a stomach turner for sure.'

Jason went on to have a major smash run at the Palladium and he reveals, 'On opening night, just before my character enters, you're up there in the dark awaiting the moment, and while I was scared I thought, well, so many of the greats have stood here and had the same feeling and, with that in mind, I figured not much could go wrong.'

It was a record breaking stint at the Palladium, which many likened to the time when fifties singer Johnny Ray performed there, with masses of young girls outside the stage door every night just waiting to glimpse their idol. Jason created even more PR for the show by arriving simply by push-bike. He told me, 'People were stunned at first that I would want to do this but, you know, I enjoyed the breeze of the city and I always travelled by my bike. I was new to theatre and had no idea about theatre people or theatre life, so when I heard I was creating a buzz and getting the show even more press I was happy. I think everyone in the show was.'

Jason left the show to great acclaim and has since appeared there to even more delight in various shows over the years, but he had one final confession about his time at the Palladium. When I asked him what happened to the famous coat that Joseph wore on stage every night, he revealed, 'Oh, that. Actually, I have it at home and it's a good diet thing, you know, because I can still get in it.

I'm not sure Lord Webber knows I still have my coat. It may be worth millions, so don't tell him, will you, Neil?' Okay, Jason, for now.

Engelbert Humperdinck
2 May 1936 – present

What a star and showman – and, of course, a massive Palladium favourite who appeared in his one and only pantomime production at the theatre, just after he found fame in the mid-sixties.

'Enge', as he is known to pals, tells me, 'I was lucky in many ways, because after the hit record, finally I was asked to appear in the Palladium panto. Now you see, today it would be unheard of for a pop star of my size at that time to do that, but then it was an honour. Although to be honest, Neil, I was nervous because, you know, I had never acted before. But my manager Gordon Mills assured me, "It will be a blast and great for your sales. Plus, you can say you appeared at the London Palladium."' Enge chuckled. 'He was very persuasive.'

The pantomime that year was *Robinson Crusoe* and it starred comedians Hope and Keen, Jimmy Logan and the brilliant Arthur Askey. It proved to be a huge box office hit that season. As Enge recalls, 'I owe all those comedians so much. I mean, I was very young but I knew how much of the trade they were teaching me – timing and how to play for laughs – a lesson in how to win over a totally different audience within minutes.'

Arthur Askey was a particular favourite to Enge. 'He was wonderful, dear Arthur, and had done so much. He could have easily not bothered about me, but he taught me a lot in a very short space of time and I was always grateful for that.'

However, it was not all plain sailing during the run. 'Poor Arthur had a terrible accident when someone left the trap door open and he fell through,' recalled Enge. 'He was out of action for a while and I know it shook him up a bit, but the show goes on and his understudy replaced him with great success.'

Enge had a favourite scene in the panto, where he was captured in dramatic action. 'Oh yes, it was the big scene before the interval and I am locked and bound in a cage on stage with all the evil things going on around me and guess what they said I should sing before the interval? You guessed it – 'Please Release Me'. It brought the house down and again, I owe that to Arthur on how to time the moment. Peak too early and you will lose the laugh, he said, but time it well and they will adore you and it will get an even bigger laugh. He was right, of course, and I did it his way every show – such wonderful memories.'

Enge revealed how he owes his huge break at the Palladium to another mega star of the golden era, though – Dickie Valentine. 'My manager Gordon Mills received a phone call from the team at *Sunday Night at the London Palladium* and they explained they were an act short because Dickie had been taken ill. Gordon instantly suggested me and they accepted. Now let me tell you, Neil, I was in shock when I got the call as this was the biggest show on TV then, the biggest thing, but Gordon was very laid back and tried to keep me happy with lines like "relax, you will be fine", "consider this your lucky charm" and all that stuff.'

Dickie Valentine was born on 4 November 1929 in London as Richard Brice. He was an actor and singer, known for his hit TV show *Calling Dickie Valentine* in 1961. He also starred in *The 6.5 Special* (1958) and *The Dickie Valentine Show* (1966). He died on 6 May 1971 in Crickhowell, Wales, after a tragic car accident, but remains today one of our best-loved singers of that generation.

Enge continued, 'So I arrive at the Palladium and outwardly played it very cool, you know, and as if this was all normal, but my tummy was churning inside. And, you know, I was warm,' he added, laughing.

The upshot was, Enge recalled, 'We did the show and those three minutes changed my life, truly, so I have the Palladium and Dickie to thank. You know, Neil, we became great friends because Dickie rang me up after watching the show to congratulate me and say how he enjoyed it. What a nice guy, eh? And we became good pals.'

Enge also let slip that the king of rock 'n' roll, the one and only Elvis Presley, was a fan of the Palladium. Elvis had been asked by Lew Grade if he would like to appear at the world famous venue and they spoke with his manager, Colonel Tom Parker, who when the offer of money came up said, 'Sure, that is good for me, but how about my boy here Elvis?' The deal never happened.

Enge told me that he would have loved to do more acting. After his stint on the Palladium stage there were offers of films and big musicals, but his music career went through the roof and he was unable to take up these offers.

He conceded, 'It's regrettable,' but with a smile, added, 'I would have loved to have gone down that track, but it was not meant to be. Of course, we all make choices and I am truly thankful that if my acting CV is left at the London Palladium in pantomime, well, it's not bad for an acting CV, now is it?'

Judy Garland
10 June 1922 – 22 June 1969

'My Mom loved the Palladium and London, in that order,' states Lorna Luft, daughter of singing legend and Palladium favourite Judy Garland.

We all know the story of the little girl called Frances Gumm who turned into the MGM star 'Judy Garland' and the lead female in such iconic hit movies as *The Wizard of Oz*, *The Clock*, *Summer Stock* and the mega classic *A Star is Born*. Described by Fred Astaire as 'the greatest entertainer who ever lived', Judy was adored by all and was tragically lost at the age of just forty-seven, after battling with drugs and alcohol.

She was a performer of such a high level that she left even her own friends and contemporaries in awe. I recall her one-time co-star Van Johnson telling a story on a chat show in the late seventies on UK TV, in which he stated that he was doing a season at the Palladium and after the show in popped Judy, with a bunch of friends that were also in London. In the number one dressing room backstage the drink, gossip and food flowed and Judy was busy telling Van just how great he was on stage.

Van recalls, 'Oh, I was telling her, "But no – honestly – no one can compare to you up there – this is your theatre," and so back and forth the compliments flew until Judy decided to say, "You know, Van, the song in your show? It's an amazing song and so hard to do. I honestly don't know how you do it."'

Van then said he began to sing it to the pals in the dressing room and within seconds the song that Judy had 'no idea' how to sing was turning into a Garland classic.

Van added, 'I was not mad with her at all, even though, like many performers, she stole my thunder. But it was Judy and she really could do a better job of most things. She had no idea of this. That is what made her endearing to her friends.'

Lorna Luft sat opposite me in the swanky surrounds of the glamorous White House Hotel in London, dressed in white and looking far younger than her years. She poured tea and told me, 'Ask away – what do you want to know? I am guessing you will ask about my show for a while and then ask more and then some more about my mother, right?' She then bellowed a laugh that shocked the entire room; she was great fun and a huge talent in her own right. It must have been difficult in the shadow of her mum, but she coped well.

Lorna is the second daughter of Judy from Judy's marriage to her then-manager Sid Luft, a man who was instrumental in making Judy a huge success here in London and at the Palladium. 'Mamma often talked about her first time here in London and just how terrified she was at the prospect of going on stage again after years in MGM movies. You see, while she had started out on the stage she had gotten used to the life of a movie star and she knew just how tough audiences can be, so she often said that "if they had booed me, I am not sure I would have come back and all because I was almost a nervous wreck about the whole thing".'

Judy, of course, was right. MGM kept the real fame of its stars secret from them by tying them down to seven-year contracts with the studio and making one film after another until their star faded and MGM boss Louis B. Mayer decided they were no longer a viable asset to the company. This is just where Judy Garland found herself in the spring of 1951.

Max Bygraves, a friend and great entertainer, told me, 'I was on the bill with her and she was terrified because, of course, she knew that this was a moment where it was make or break and basically the press had not been kind already about her. She came over on the *Queen Mary* and to see Hollywood stars back then was a rare thing, in the sense that they did not pop over all the time like they do now. When Judy disembarked they had already decided that, at a mere twenty-eight years old, she was in fact past her best. Judy herself admitted that she might have picked the wrong outfit.'

'She came onto the stage and was very nervous,' Max told me, 'which stunned all of us, really, and then she launched into her song. She was wearing this yellow creation, which seemed to drown her, but not her voice. After the first song the audience were on their feet – a standing ovation – it brought tears of relief to the eyes of Judy. She went to take a bow, tripped up, and fell over. A silence ensued and then she got up, kicked off her too-high heels and spoke to the audience in the Palladium as if they were her new best friends – it was amazing.'

'Mom thought she had blown it when she tripped up,' Lorna told me, 'but she was goofy like – that is what her fans liked about her, the fact she was touchable and yet untouchable at the same time.'

Lorna said that her mom loved the whole season at the Palladium and she became the toast of the town. She added, 'You see, Mom was a tad down in the dumps, really. I mean, her movie career looked like it was over and then she comes here to the UK and wonders if she can win them over. So her stint at the Palladium gave her, quite simply, her confidence back and she thanked the theatre and the people for that, she truly did.'

The London Palladium was indeed a second home to the legend of Judy Garland. Season after season followed and her popularity soared again. She even made part of her hit movie *I Could Go on Singing* at the theatre, at her insistence. She told producers, 'I think it's the only place on earth where I actually feel alive, right there on that stage.'

Judy also famously went onto to host the showbiz career of her first daughter Liza (Minnelli) at the Palladium, in a series of concerts called 'Judy and Liza at the London Palladium'.

I met Liza and she told me, 'You see, that show right there in that theatre was a turning point for Mom because at the start of the show I was a kid, you know, having a go and doing okay, with my mom stood in the wings urging me on and shouting all the time; but in that theatre I became an entertainer and she knew it, from just urging me on. She got to thinking that maybe I could be some kind of threat, seriously, and the mood changed as my applause from the crowd got more and more. I left the wings looking at my mom but boy, when she came on the stage to meet me she came on not as my mom but as Judy Garland. Do you know how terrifying that was?' she asked, laughing.

Judy Garland may have seen the Palladium as her true showbiz home but it was also the scene of one of her last ever appearances.

In the spring of 1969, she was invited by the producers to appear on the hit show *Sunday Night at the London Palladium*. Shirley Bassey was also on the bill and was meant to close the show.

Judy looked frail and unwell, but Bassey later said, 'I knew that we were in the presence of a star, and I mean a star, so naturally I suggested that she closed the show and she did. And you know what? As she sang, all the frailness slipped away and the legend that we all knew and loved simply came back and it was a wonder to see.'

'I loathe the way people look at my mom as a victim,' Lorna told me, 'because when I watch that taped show of her with my sister at the Palladium that is the real mother of mine up there. I often go past the theatre myself and just take a little time to remember her there, because she was always truly happy on the Palladium stage – she told me that often.'

It was in her London mews flat that Judy stumbled into her bathroom late one night and died of an overdose of barbiturates, on 22 June 1969 at the age of forty-seven. Her daughter Liza Minnelli paid for her funeral, and her former lover James Mason delivered her touching eulogy. She is still an icon to this day due to her famous performances in *The Wizard of Oz* (1939), *Meet Me in St. Louis* (1944), *Easter Parade* (1948) and *A Star Is Born* (1954).

Mickey Rooney
23 September 1920 – 6 April 2014

Mickey Rooney does not have the greatest Palladium memory but, having interviewed him numerous times, on visits to the UK and while working in the US, he always stuck to his story that his big Argyll Street flop was, as ever, not his doing.

Mickey Rooney was short in height but massive in talent. While he started out in vaudeville (a genre of variety entertainment), he found fame in the movies, first during the silent era and then as the all-singing all-dancing star of some wonderful MGM classic musicals alongside Judy Garland. Mickey had a longer, if more volatile, career than Judy.

'I remember being in the President of the United States' Oval Office. I was just nineteen years old,' Mickey said, 'when he told me I was the most famous person in the US and also the world.' There was no irony in his voice. He fully believed many of the stories he reeled off during our meetings together and who was I to tell him that they were untrue?

Mickey liked to regale the story of how he found and named Marilyn Monroe and even composed tunes for her.

'She was beautiful but not stunning, as she later became,' he said. 'Marilyn was hanging around with an agent pal of mine called Johnny Hyde and it was him and me that decided the path of her career – honestly, it's true. I suggested that she be called Marilyn after an old MGM star Marilyn Miller and came up with stories for the press.'

Mickey had many tales like this and discussing them was always fun, but when I broached the thorny topic of his Palladium debut in the late forties he always managed to sidestep the tale until one day I just said, 'Look, why not set the record straight about just what happened?' And so, after a deep breath, he told me why – in his own words – he was not the glittering success that he had and should have been.

By the late forties Mickey's film career as the golden boy of Hollywood was over. He was fired from the top studio of MGM because the boss Louis B. Mayer decided that he was now too old (and perhaps too much trouble) to star in the Andy Hardy movies. The studio cut him loose from a lucrative contract after tolerating years of frequent tardiness, gambling and, of course, his love of women. Mickey did love women and would go on to marry eight times, his most famous wife being the luscious Ava Gardener, who was his co-worker at the time and Mayer's prize star for the future.

'Marrying Ava was the beginning of the end for me regards the career at MGM,' Mickey told me, 'because, while we were in love, she was not considered suitable for me as the character I played on screen. Basically I called him (Mayer) out and demanded that I be allowed to marry her.' MGM relented, but of course Mayer was right. The marriage was almost over before it had begun, but, as Mickey recalled with a chuckle, 'Everything was taken over by the studio, clothes, pictures and press releases. Even the vows were written by a script writer on the lot.'

MGM's PR machine had spun his stories and movies around more than a few times and it was ready to let him go. After that, Mickey worked for any studio or stage that would hire him as a matter of need rather than desire. He admitted, 'I was hopeless with money because as a kid I figured the money would go on forever and ever, which of course it did not. I only have myself to blame.'

In the latter part of 1948 Mickey received an offer to appear for a season at the world famous London Palladium. He seized the opportunity; at that time it was a familiar offer to the Hollywood masses. 'I was told that my star still shone brightly here in the United Kingdom,' he said. 'So even though I had not appeared on a stage for over twenty years, I was low on money and had nothing much else happening – it made me think that this might kickstart my career back on the screen too.'

Arriving in England, Mickey found that the warm welcome was indeed warm and he was on a high. 'I was the toast of London prior to opening. I thought this was great and yes, I took full advantage of what London had to offer. I thought, because I was being fussed over and interviewed, that success at the theatre could not be that hard. I was wrong, because all my bad press of being axed from the studio and that sort of stuff had filtered through. I had no idea just how bad it was going to get.'

Mickey was sketchy at first about just what his act entailed but he told me that it was a smash when he arranged it back in New York. 'We knew we had something and I know that people maybe were expecting me doing some film stuff and maybe Judy coming over, but I did explain to the managers what I had in mind and yes, the show was good.'

Mickey, though, failed to mention that the pre-publicity had done nothing to help his box office. As he was booked for a season he had hoped that the opening night would turn things around. 'Why wouldn't it happen?' he said. 'I am Mickey Rooney.'

The opening night was less than brilliant, with Mickey throwing everything he had into his act, including drumming, singing, dancing, stories from his film career and even a skirt. 'After all,' he told me, 'Danny Kaye did almost the same show and became a smash, so why not me?'

Sadly, his confidence was misguided. After two weeks playing to less than full houses, Mickey had to pull out. His dream of a dazzling comeback was in tatters.

Speaking in 2007 – more than fifty years after his experience – Mickey told me on tape, 'You know I lied there because, well, I was advised to get ill, as it were, and so I did. I mean, by this point what was there to lose? Anyway, back then I really was ill through stress and money worries, so yeah, my Palladium dream was over.'

Not quite, though, because Mickey then went on to tell me how his onetime co-star Judy Garland tried and failed to persuade him to come back to the Palladium later in the fifties and sixties in her various shows. 'I would have loved it, to be honest, and it was something that we discussed, but you know something? I had an ego and my idea was that we took a half of the show each. Naturally Judy did not need me – I needed her – but my ego told me a cameo in the show – a song or two – would not be enough. I have never told anyone that, really, but it's true. So the idea of me and Judy back together at the Palladium never took off. She was naturally great about it though and told me that if I don't do a full show then my fans won't be happy with me and I can't risk that, now can I? She was right, of course,' laughed Mickey.

Mickey was to have his day at the Palladium – a very true story to tell – when he was invited to appear on the stage with his former MGM co-star Ann Miller. The pair had teamed up to star in a mega smash-hit musical, *Sugar Babies*, at the Savoy Theatre. The show was playing to packed houses and producers at the Palladium were keen to include a 'snippet' performance.

Mickey was over the moon with the offer, but told me the real lure was meeting the British royal family. 'I adored them, so how could I refuse?' he said. 'I agreed to give the Palladium one more go.'

Producers at the Savoy were keen to avoid disruption to their own schedule, not least with enthused audiences and a hefty pay package for Mickey and Ann. They requested that they hit the Palladium early in the evening so they could rush back to the Savoy in good time.

Mickey recalled, 'I was annoyed by this at first. My huge concern was that we would appear and never get to meet them (the royals) at the end of the show – but then the sweetener was that Ann and I would be presented to Her Majesty prior to the show. Ann would present the flowers and I would present the programme. We knocked that out and I heard back from the Palace that they loved us both. I still have the letter – so, rightly so, while it may not have started off well for me at the Palladium, the old girl did me proud in the end.'

One final meeting with Mickey left me wondering if he was going to be all right. After the launch of his panto stint we went outside and he asked me if I could buy him a ice cream as he was banned from having one by his wife due to being on a diet.

We went around the corner to the shop and, while Mickey was looking in the ice cream cart and grumbling, the young girl asked me about him and said, 'Ah, is that your granddad then?'

I hastily replied, 'Oh no, it's Mickey Rooney.' She just smiled and took the money. Outside the store he was standing there looking like a young boy eating his ice cream when he turned all serious and said, 'Neil, can I trust you?'

'Of course,' I replied. 'What is it?'

Mickey then went on to tell me that he was being blackmailed by one close member of his family. He said that he was scared and had no idea what to do – could I help him? He began to cry and was getting really upset, like a spoilt child, as he felt I was not taking him seriously.

As we began to climb the stairs back to the studio he repeated it all again and said, 'Please don't leave me. Can you come back to the hotel with me, please?'

I did find this strange, as he was only with his wife, who seemed charming and kind, even though he referred to her as 'wife number eight'. She would then joke, 'Final wife, Mickey,' which left me confused, a bit, as she seemed to be getting annoyed with that comment.

After we got him in the car he asked for my mobile number and begged me to leave my phone on. I did, and within a few hours Mickey was on the phone asking me to call the police after what he had told me. I really did not believe what he was saying, to be honest, and so I put it down to him being old and infirm.

A week later I am walking to Fox News in New York when I pass the newspaper stand. It screams in loud black print, 'Mickey Rooney Blackmail Plot by Family.' I literally stood still and could hardly believe it – Mickey had been telling the truth after all. It just goes to show you that in this job you have to take some things seriously.

Mickey Rooney, whose career spanned nine decades, died in his Los Angeles home on 6 April 2014 at the age of ninety-three. In his autobiography, *Life Is Too Short*, he said, 'Had I been brighter, the ladies been gentler, the liquor weaker, the gods kinder, and the dice hotter – it might have all ended up in a one-sentence story.'

Dean Martin and Jerry Lewis
7 June 1917 – 25 December 1995 and 16
March 1926 – present

I was sitting opposite Ricci Martin, the son of the legendary entertainer Dean Martin. He was pleasant and, although good-looking with a very easy charm, it's not until the studio floor manager shouts, 'Action!' that he snaps into character. In the bat of an eye he becomes his famous father's son.

Naturally I was keen to hear all about the singer and actor who is, without doubt, one of the greatest entertainers that has graced the Palladium stage. Ricci oozes names from a golden age of Hollywood; Sinatra, Sammy and Judy and more, but to him they were 'dad's pals, not superstars of the world stage'.

Ricci was in London to promote his own one-man show, based on his father's life, and he told me his memories of coming to London with his father as a child. 'Oh, he loved London and the people of England,' he said, 'but it took a while, you know, when Dad first came here. He and Jerry, although they were big stars on the silver screen, were not that popular when they took to the stage of the Palladium, which left Dad baffled.

'It was 1953 when the boys decided to have a go at the London stage and they were buoyed up by the fact that their pals like Judy, Frank and Danny Kaye all came back saying how well they had gone and what an opportunity there was to be had. Sure enough, even their movie producer, Hall Wallis, told them to go; after all, it could not harm the movies they were making.' He went on, 'They had a great act, which was a smash at the Paramount in New York. Of course they thought they could do the same in London, but they had not bothered to ask which bits of their act had gone down well and which had not – even Danny Kaye had changed his act to suit the British audiences – so they flew off to England high on hope.'

As reports show, when Dean and Jerry arrived in town for their season at the theatre it was like the arrival of a pop star, with the media of the day going nuts and talking about Dean's good looks and Jerry's crew cut. The press was encouraging and those with tickets were full of anticipation. Dean and Jerry believed the hype and enjoyed many events and nights out prior to the show opening. The good times were shortlived.

'Something went so wrong between arriving in town and arriving on that stage. Dad told me, "You know, we did everything we could to make these people love us and while we got laughs we knew, oh, we knew, that we were in trouble with the audience." Like all acts they figured it would get better as the week went on, until the reviews came in.'

Looking back at the reviews today, it's hard to believe the comedy duo could have got it so wrong. Praise was hard to find – no one seemed to like the act – just a few being vaguely kind about Dean's singing and the general fooling around. The die was cast and basically the boys tanked at the box office. It became the show to avoid that season at the Palladium.

Despite the disappointment, Dean told Ricci, 'It was a hard lesson – the whole trip. Our regional shows were not a glittering success either, even though our agents said we would do better in the provinces. Boy, we did not, and it dented our confidence for years, basically.'

As part of their Palladium deal, Dean and Jerry had to tour other Moss Empire theatres – the regional shows – including the dreaded Glasgow Empire. The tour was not going well but a strange thing happened in Glasgow, as Ricci recalls. 'I know Dad loved the Scots. He often told me they had a great sense of humour and they totally got their act. The press was against them and they had offended dignitaries and so forth by turning up late to events, but their hotel (the now famous Central Hotel in Glasgow) was still mobbed nightly.'

They may have struggled at the Palladium and faced plenty of negative press, but the duo floored the Scots – they loved the show – and it boosted their confidence no end. Yet this boost was shortlived, as Ricci tells me. 'When Dad got back to the US he was quoted as saying, "British critics stink." He may have thought that privately, but Dad told me he never actually said it. The studio Paramount issued a statement of denial but the damage was done.'

So it was a volatile experience for Dean and Jerry in the UK. Dean never quite got over his initial reception at the Palladium but he grew fond of the venue over the years, as Ricci remembers. 'He loved performing there and filmed some specials later on and generally had a good time. His fans remained loyal and things were always pretty great for him, so I know while it may have started off badly both he and the venue came good in the end.'

Dean Martin died on Christmas morning in 1995, at the age of seventy-eight, in Beverly Hills, California. Martin is regarded as a legendary screen and stage performer and is best known for his comedic partnership with Jerry Lewis, as well as for his participation in the iconic Rat Pack.

Joe Church
30 November 1919 – 15 September 1999

I must be honest and admit that I was unfamiliar with the name Joe Church before I met him at a theatrical garden party. Like all good variety stars, Joe soon put me right about his popularity and frequent appearances at the Palladium.

Joe had a rare insight on the billing during the 1950s – the same era as Dean and Jerry – and his story offers an unusual take on the buildup to each show and the PR machine of the theatre.

Joe remembered heading backstage for a press call with the boys, only to find himself in front of the very sexy blonde bombshell Diana Dors who was, at the time, a huge star contracted to Rank Film. She was known as 'Britain's Marilyn Monroe'.

'Oh we were all agog when she came down to the stage door,' smiled Joe. 'She was an amazing-looking woman and a gifted comedian herself, plus she had charm, and lots of it. The real problem was that she stole the headlines in the press and that was something else that Jerry did not take too kindly to. You think they only do that kind of PR stuff today but getting Diana back then was seen as a real gem. There was talk of her also coming onto the show to do a skit with the boys but I don't think it happened.'

'The problem with the duo (Dean and Jerry) is that they never really understood the humour of us Brits,' Joe continued. 'Sure, we loved them on the big screen and their films were very popular but unlike, say, Danny Kaye, who I also loved, I think the boys thought their fame would simply be enough. Dean was smart and a very classy guy; he had that wonderful singing voice and he knew it, of course, whereas with Jerry, not a lot of people responded well to his clowning around and in turn their act suffered and they both knew it. I liked them though and wished them well. I mean, to me they were huge stars and deserved a bigger chance at the Palladium. I know they were both sore about their time there.'

Jane McDonald
4 April 1963 – present

Yorkshire lass Jane may be best known as a *Loose Women* and reality TV star who found fame on the TV show *The Cruise*, but, like all performers, she went down the tough path of working men's clubs to earn her place at the Mecca of show business – the Palladium.

She felt she had finally 'arrived' when she took the stage with her own show, and told me, 'I think you have to be a performer to fully understand what it means to someone to land that venue. I mean, I had hired it, so I knew a lot was riding on me to deliver. I kept thinking about how

I would be standing right there in the spotlight that had shone on so many of the people I admired, but yes, I was there and I was doing it.'

Echoing the words of many who land the Palladium, Jane said she can feel something special when there. 'It does have a magic, without a doubt. I mean, you have to believe it does, but I do. And even backstage or just getting ready in the room you think, my goodness, Frank Sinatra has stood in this spot and done the same thing as me – maybe not as nervous – but yeah, the magic was there and still is each time I go back. Wherever you play in the world, there is no place like the biggest venue back home. Appearing at the Palladium really helped me in Las Vegas and other places because it's so well-known and people just respect it. I think so many performers owe it a debt.'

Bill Kenwright CBE
4 September 1945 – present

'I still get a thrill when I see a poster outside the theatre and I look up and it says "Bill Kenwright presents …",' Bill tells me.

Lancashire lad Bill Kenwright CBE fronts one of the UK's largest independent theatre and film production companies under his own name. His experience is second to none and has earned him an enviable accreditation above or beside the door of many of London's top theatres, including the Palladium.

Meetings with the impresario are always loaded with chat, gossip and wonderful stories that offer a unique glimpse into the business of production and performance.

Bill started his professional life as an actor. He was signed by Granada TV in the sixties to play the handsome Gordon Clegg, son of Betty the famous hotpot maker on *Coronation Street*. His fame, for a while, was that of a pop star and he loved it.

'Oh, I did,' he smiles, 'because while I enjoyed acting I had always, I suppose, loved the idea of being a pop star and my hero was Tommy Steele. To me he was bigger than Elvis because he was "ours". So when I got to the soap level of fame, sure, I did enjoy it – I was just touching the level of adoration that Tom received and it was a fine place to be in.'

Bill had foresight, though, and he admitted that he had no idea whether his role on the soap was secure or if they would just kill him off.

'*Coronation Street* was huge, and I mean huge, at that time, to the point where if my mum went into the Co-op to get some ham or something all the women would want to stop and gossip or tell her off because of what I was doing on screen. The show was wonderful because it was real lives and real people for the first time on TV, which until then it had all been posh types. So yeah, a great time for me to appear in a show like that but I knew I also wanted to produce and direct at some point.'

Bill, along with an actor pal, decided to team up and form their own repertory. 'It was a chance to give other actors work, say when they were out of a series like a soap. It was a great success but, you know, I always dreamed – and I say dreamed – that one day I would be able to bring my shows to the Palladium, but I never thought I would. I mean, I was just a TV actor. Thanks to lots of hard work and making great friends like Lord Webber, I have been a regular here for years, but I don't get complacent. You see, this is the greatest theatre in the world, without a doubt, and I think you owe it to the theatre and the public to put on the best possible production you can. I always say to my team, "Remember, this is for the Palladium," and we are "proud to present"; I really am totally in love with the place.'

Barry Manilow
7 June 1943 – present

I asked Barry Manilow what he thought about the Palladium. He got all sweet and quite teary. 'Oh my, the Palladium. Where do I start? Boy, this is one tough question – give me a moment.'

Barry Manilow is a wonderful guy, bursting with talent and pure showbiz gold. Whenever he decides to entertain in London his loyal and adoring fans offer their support unconditionally.

What you see is what you get with Barry – 'music and passion are always in fashion'. I have interviewed him on numerous occasions and he is flawlessly well groomed, charming and appreciative.

Barry has appeared on the world's greatest stages, including London's Palladium. He never seems to take it for granted, telling me, 'You know, Neil, the thing about that theatre is it's got life, you know what I'm saying? There is something about it, and I don't just mean all the people that have appeared there – it is a magic spot.

'I have never told anyone this before but sometimes I like to visit the theatre alone. I know people may find that odd but there is nothing nicer than, say, going in early one Sunday morning and soaking up the atmosphere of the greats – the greats that have been on that stage long before you and me were even thought of,' he laughs. 'I just love doing that and you get inspired, because all has gone before you and if you're lucky enough to get on that stage then you'd sure better deliver, because it deserves it and you do too, for your own level as a professional. So yeah, that is my secret; I have visited when the place is almost dark and just soaked up the atmosphere. It never fails me.'

On the day we spoke, Barry was appearing in a Royal Variety show live from the Palladium. He dazzled in his sequined red jacket and looked every inch the star he is. He wowed the crowd and delivered a spectacular performance that deserved its standing ovation. I like to think he stood there listening to the applause and soaking up everything his Palladium had to offer.

Barry Humphries CBE
17 February 1934 – present

The quietly spoken Barry Humphries was born in Melbourne, Australia, and has captured the very essence of variety by giving us two of the funniest yet contrasting characters for stage: Dame Edna Everage and Sir Les Patterson.

Dame Edna is a joyously boisterous global icon with almost regal appeal who dazzles audiences with her glittering outfits, lilac bouffant hair, curt humour and gladiolus giveaways. Sir Les is an obese rebel with a vagabond-like appearance and unlikely appeal, who shocks with his booze-stained suits, crooked teeth, dubious grey flick and lecherous offensive wit.

They are extraordinary extremes, yet pure 'variety' genius. Indeed, Dame Edna is perhaps the only act in the history of the Royal Variety show at the Palladium to successfully gatecrash the royal box with a royal audience *in situ* – a truly classic moment for audiences around the world.

Barry's early road to stardom was a tough one, though, enduring many nights of stand up, all manner of TV shows, radio and of course a foray into films, but he always had the Palladium in mind. 'Back home in Australia the Palladium was the showbiz Mecca, simple as that, really. I mean, you had made it if you got there and I was determined to make that stage where I had seen the greats.'

So how did Dame Edna and Sir Les finally get through UK Border Control and on to the great stage of the Palladium?

Preparing for his final show there in early 2014, Barry told me, 'People think that Edna was this creation instantly liked, but at first she was more of a sour creation, you know, not the housewife superstar that we all know and love today. It was here in the UK that people decided to take me to their bosom and where Dame Edna flourished. It's been a great career and I have a lot to thank this theatre for. What better and fitting place to say farewell – for now, anyway,' he laughs.

Few will forget 'that' moment – Royal Variety show, November 2013 – when Dame Edna slid confidently into the royal box, looked at Camilla and Prince Charles, checked the prince's ticket and in true Dame Edna fashion smiled and announced, 'It's okay; they have found me a better seat.'

'Of course, this brought down the house at the Palladium,' said Barry. 'I owe the theatre a lot, as they totally went with it and helped me create some Palladium history. I know Dame Edna was pleased,' he adds with a wink.

Robbie Williams
13 February 1974 – present

Robbie Williams is a pop icon and true showman, known for his antics with Take That and his successful solo career. He has international acclaim, which is almost global, 'Apart from the US,' he admits. 'They don't want to know there.'

Nonetheless, with roaring success at home, Robbie made sure he got his dream when he recorded a TV special at the Palladium for his swing album, *Swings Both Ways*, in November 2013.

'We decided it had to come from the Palladium,' he told me, 'because the greats like Nat King Cole, Sinatra, Dean and Sammy had all appeared there and that was what the album was about, really – bringing that music back to life in its spiritual home. So we drew up a concept of how we fancied the show to be and you know me, it had to be glitter and glam.

'It was a dream come true. No, really – the show, the place, the audience and the atmosphere. I had it recorded by the BBC and I thought, my goodness, you know how old-school is this – me with top hat and tails on – but it was a great moment for me and I knew that I had become a entertainer at that point, not just a pop star.'

Robbie also appeared in the Royal Variety show that year with Olly Murs (*X Factor* runner up). Talking fondly of Olly, Robbie said, 'He was young and not really that fazed, so you know, I became the dad and explained what an honour it was that we were there together. Of course, he looks at me like I'm, well, slightly mad. But I know that in years to come, like me, he will be able to watch himself up there on that stage and think, well, I did it – I played the Palladium. So maybe I made his dream come true, too.'

Sir Norman Wisdom
4 February 1915 – 4 October 2010

Sir Norman Wisdom – just the name can bring a smile of affection. He had that effect throughout his career, which endured until retirement at the staggering age of ninety. He was a celebrated regular at the Palladium and we should never forget the Sunday night show in 1961 when he teamed up with Bruce Forsyth to fill almost an entire hour-long programme with the notorious 'Wallpaper Sketch'.

He loved the Palladium and retained a photo from the 1950s, showing an eager audience and fan base waiting to see him outside the theatre. He was thrilled with that picture.

When Sir Norman was around, the world seemed a better place – even Charlie Chaplin described him as his 'favourite clown' – and many others just adored his tomfoolery humour and consistent charms on screen, on stage and, for those lucky enough to meet him, in person.

Sir Norman was born in London on 4 February 1915 and enjoyed great success with a series of comedy films, produced between 1953 and 1966 and featuring his hapless character Norman Pitkin. He also caused a riot in the 1965 Rank film *The Early Bird*, which became his most successful film ever.

His success and celebrity spread across borders, with some unexpected 'breaks' in territories such as South America, the Middle East and Albania, where he was considered a comic king. He landed roles on Broadway and was later back on screen with an acclaimed part in the TV play *Going Gently* (1981), where he won hearts with his portrayal of a dying cancer patient. Many will also remember his roles in *Last of the Summer Wine* and, briefly, in *Coronation Street*.

His longevity was outstanding and was rightly recognised with an OBE in 1995 and knighthood in 2000.

I never once in my wildest dreams thought that I would get to meet Sir Norman, yet alone consider him as a personal family friend – a true variety blessing.

I was asked by a TV channel to 'interview one of your favourite stars', with guaranteed publishing, regardless of who I chose. I wanted to wow the editor, but this opportunity was at short notice and I was struggling to pin down an act.

I glanced down the listings guide to find that the great Norman Wisdom (not yet a 'Sir' at this time) was in town and preparing to launch his new movie *Adam & Evil* at Pinewood Studios. He was expected to co-star with seventies sex bomb Bo Derek.

Now remember, I had never done this type of interview before, so with great nerves I called the production office and bleated out that I would require an interview. The cheek, eh? Well, I was lucky to be connected with Norman's right-hand man and PR manager for thirty-eight years, Phil Day, who was in fact kindness itself. Phil told me that Norman would be available and that he would meet me at the very plush Langham Hotel, opposite the BBC in London.

I worried so much prior to the interview, as this was the big one. Norman Wisdom was a huge star; he was the biggest box office draw in the UK at the time and had a number one record. I could hardly contain my excitement when the day arrived.

I got to the hotel early to make sure that I had a good seat for him and waited – or fidgeted – in the reception area. I heard a rustle at the rotating doors – you know, the posh ones with uniformed doormen outside. I knew straight away that the funny man had arrived. He had got himself tangled up in the doors and had simply brought the hotel to a standstill. Pulling himself free, he promptly marched up to me and tripped in the only way he could. Unfazed, he said, 'I'm Norman, you're Neil, right?' Bliss – we were off.

I could not get a word in, but it was glorious. He was reeling off one great story after another, so who cared? 'Did I tell you about the time Marilyn Monroe kissed me?' he asked. 'How about me and Sean Connery? I was a bigger box office draw than him, you know.'

Norman had me enthralled and then, with a stroke of kindness, he said we should order lunch. I gulped; after all, the editor had just pulled the expenses and if the great Norman was to have ordered big then it was up to me, with very little money on board, to pay for it.

Norman looked at the menu with longing, then slammed it shut and announced, 'It's a bit posh in here, innit? There's a café nearby – smashing eggs and chips – come on.' So off we tottered and, true to form, he had the whole café in stitches within minutes of our arrival.

I later found out that Norman was aware that this was my big break and also that I had very little cash. He treated me to lunch and I felt exceptionally privileged as we toasted our new-found friendship with lemonade (we were both non-drinkers). He then said, 'Back to the hotel,' for the picture. 'It will look better in a swanky place, mate.'

I received a call that evening. 'Hi, it's Norman. Just checking that you got all you needed today.' I couldn't believe it. I assured him I did and thanked him for being so generous with his time. He told me some more hilarious stories and then how he would be attending a showbiz event later in the year and if I was there I would see him again. He signed off and I was left beaming. How did that just happen?

I did indeed attend the showbiz event – Norman was the star guest – and I was able to introduce to him Alan Scott and Ann Montini (my mother and father) who were great fans.

We kept in touch with Sir Norman for many years – 'Call anytime,' he said generously – and one day he announced he was on his way to Mirfield, our home town. A new scheme had been established in UK libraries, offering the general public access to Norman's biggest films on loan.

A healthy eighty years old by this stage, he still had everyone at the library in stitches, swinging off a lamppost, telling stories and answering questions with unrivalled wit. It was a busy day, yet he still had time to join us at home for tea and sandwiches.

I have been lucky to bump into Sir Norman on so many occasions over the years, partly due to my media career and working as a showbiz reporter for Sky News but also as a friend. I even got to work with him briefly at the Grand Theatre in Blackpool, where he was also guest starring on a live show for the National Lottery.

By this stage, I had unknowingly made the assumption that Sir Norman was bursting with confidence – riding on an unbreakable wave of variety success that just came naturally to him – but I was about to learn something interesting.

After the lottery show we went across to the Imperial Hotel for a gossip over lemonade, and Sir Norman asked me, 'Was it ok? Did it go well?' He stopped me in my tracks and I pondered over this seemingly simple yet very revealing question. 'Did it go well?'

This is how Sir Norman remained at the top of his game. He never took his success for granted and I bet he never took a venue, an audience, a friend or a colleague for granted either. I bet he cherished the magic of each regional theatre as much as the Palladium, although even he might admit the Palladium holds a special place in his heart.

Of course, that hunger to make sure people laughed was there regardless of theatre or territory, stage or screen, but his unassuming approach and occasional need for reassurance demonstrated the humble side we came to love so much.

Sir Norman would always say goodbye with a 'keep laughing' and yet, perhaps ironically, he had his biggest hit with a track he wrote called 'Don't Laugh at Me'. The thing is, we did laugh at him and, thanks to his wonderful legacy, I think it will always be that way.

We should all be grateful for Sir Norman Wisdom, the little man with a big talent and an even bigger heart. He is surely sorely missed, but imagine the havoc he is now causing upstairs.

Tommy Steele OBE
17 December 1936 – present

Tommy Steele OBE is yet another of our greatest variety stars. Even as a small child he delighted audiences with a series of spectacular no-expense-spared TV specials. Tommy really has done it all, both at home and abroad – including a record run at the Palladium. He was considered by many to be Britain's first real rock 'n' roll star and also flourished on musical stage (*Half a Sixpence* and *Singin' in the Rain*) and across the Atlantic in Hollywood films (*Happiest Millionaire* and *Finian's Rainbow*).

Like others, I had been in awe of him for many years and hoped that my media career and role as an entertainment reporter for CBS News and Sky News would one day lead to the chance of a meeting. Well, late in the day during the winter of 2009 the telephone rang – it was the glamorous PR guru and friend to the stars, Jackie Gill.

'Hello Neil, would you like to interview Tommy Steele?' And it got better. 'It's at the London Palladium and you will be the only TV station there.' The rest of the conversation went by in a haze.

Universal records had finally seen the light and decided to put out a huge double CD of Tommy's hits including 'Rock with the Cavemen', 'Butter Fingers' and 'Little White Bull'.

I was to meet him in the Cinderella Bar, which was filled with the sound of his music and adorned with posters depicting his many films – who could forget *The Tommy Steele Story*? While I have interviewed some of the biggest names in variety showbiz, there is nothing quite like meeting a genuine home-grown talent. This was a Sir Norman Wisdom moment, for sure, and I was excited.

Tommy's arrival was announced with a professional ease by musical impresario and great chum Bill Kenwright, and he could not have been nicer. Some stars get fed up with setting the camera or sound prior to interview, but not Mr Steele, who was full of quips and laughs as we prepared to get down to serious business – well, sort of.

Tommy explained that he never saw himself as a rival to Elvis at all. 'All that was kind of put about by the press. It helped, of course, but I know we both admired each other and that was enough for me.'

I asked Tommy about his early recordings for Decca. 'It was funny, really, as it was all so new. I mean, pop music was new, I was pop music,' he laughed. 'We did four songs a day and they were normally recorded live. To me, a nineteen-year-old lad from South London, well, it was beyond a dream.'

Tommy also revealed that he got paid around 4p per single. 'People may laugh at that now but there was in fact no marketing. It was variety agents that really held the strings then and they would book you on to variety shows all around the country – big summer shows in Blackpool, where you would be on the bill with comics, dancers and magicians. Now, while I was top of the bill, I was keener to see the other acts as they were new and exciting to me. I adored travelling around the UK and staying in digs. I was young, what was not to like?'

Even at the height of his fame Tommy relished doing panto, something that today's pop stars at his level would probably balk at. 'It was expected, really,' he said. 'I mean, when I was number three in the charts with 'Butter Fingers', I was in panto at the Liverpool Empire singing it three times daily and shooting off to appear on a TV show, say, on the Sunday in London. It was not deemed uncool in them days. You were glad of the work and the long run they gave you.'

Tommy laughs at the very first time he appeared on a TV show. 'Jack Payne was hosting the show – *Off the Record*, and he wore a big heavy woollen suit, totally looking odd against me, like – and he said, "Now here is Tommy Steele to sing; it's not my sort of music, but there you go," and bang, I was on.'

While his parents were proud of Tommy's early success, they waited three years until they saw him on the TV. He explained, 'Well, no one had one (a TV) around our way and while the local pub had one it was upstairs in their private quarters. Even the Royal Variety was still in its infancy, TV-wise, but my family was fit to burst when we got on there, like – people forget nowadays that the scene was new, totally new, and so there were no set rules.'

After Tommy's appeal came the Skiffle Sessions and then the Beatles, but he was well into his musical variety stage by then and clocking up the longest run by anyone at his beloved London Palladium. That record still holds and hence it was the chosen venue for this very special interview.

Finally, I asked him what the future holds and he turned to me to reveal, 'I love to work, but you can't do big TV specials now, they simply can't afford to make them – they can't afford to repeat them. It costs too much, I mean, paying the royalties of the orchestra alone – thirty-six musicians in total – would be massive.'

So today Tommy, who belies his years and has the energy of a twenty-year-old, settles for opportunities to thrill his fans as and when they suit. He recently played a wonderful Ebenezer Scrooge in Bill Kenwright's totally delicious production of *Scrooge* – and, of course, it was staged at the Palladium before enjoying a successful regional tour (finishing January 2014). As ever, Tommy made the part his very own.

You know, they say in showbiz that you should never meet your heroes, but I shall always remember my afternoon of pure delight with the legend that is Tommy Steele.

Aled Jones MBE
29 December 1970 – present

We all remember Aled Jones as the angel-faced boy who rose to fame singing 'Walking in the Air', the famous soundtrack to the 1982 film adaptation of *The Snowman*. Since then, Aled has become a household name and master of variety trades; singer, author, TV presenter and even solo host of his own chat show. He has earned his place at the Palladium but the true value of the experience took a while to sink in.

'I don't mean this glibly,' he told me, 'but I was doing so much at that time that I suppose I did not take it all in before the show. For sure I knew it was the world famous theatre and there had been many greats before me and all that – but you know, when you're young things tend to glide over you, don't they?'

Reminiscing, he concedes, 'It was a huge deal, looking back now. Oh yes, a career highlight; even now it sends a shiver through me. You're right that every performer dreams of appearing there and the moment should be cherished. In this job it just may never happen again.' But, as ever with Aled, good things just keep on coming.

Aled was awarded an MBE in the 2013 Queen's Birthday Honours List for his services to music and broadcasting and for charitable services. His story will no doubt continue.

Stan Boardman
7 December 1940 – present

Stan was born on Merseyside and really set his heart on playing professional football for Liverpool. After failing to make the grade in big time soccer, he made a hit in the haulage business.

'I needed a steady job but I always found the time to make the men laugh. It was like an inbuilt thing for me,' he told me. His persistence was to pay off when he won a Butlins holiday camp talent contest in 1976 – an accolade even he muses at.

'I don't know if you would call it dim or brave but somehow I decided to enter the talent show on camp,' Stan recalls. 'It's hard to imagine now, but these events were huge, like, and when you think about it, very cheap for Butlins as the campers were entertaining themselves. I clubbed together an act and somehow won the first prize. Trust me, I was as stunned as anyone – but it gave me the bug.'

That talent contest was just one of many in a much larger national competition. Stan, now gaining in style and mastering better gags with each appearance, progressed through to a place in the grand final at the London Palladium.

It was here that his distinctive style of comedy and his original material helped him walk off with the £1,000 first prize, a summer season engagement and the title 'Star Act of the Year'. 'Can you believe it?' Stan asked. 'I mean, that takes some beating, don't you think, as a Palladium story? It was great fun and I don't recall that much about the event as we were told to treat the stage like you would at any Butlins – can you imagine that? I mean there is some difference between the ballroom at Butlins and the stage of the London Palladium.

'I got a Cup, of course, but the best thing was the prize money – it helped pay off some of my debts – and the whole experience was the start of my career. You never get over walking on that stage,' Stan added. 'It makes you feel you have arrived and it proves that the theatre is not at all bothered about where you come from, because if you can make them laugh then you're on – simple as that.'

Mike Reid
19 January 1940 – 29 July 2007

The Butlins talent contest was a huge event for the London Palladium and far more prestigious than today's *X Factor* or *Britain's Got Talent*.

Mike Reid, who I interviewed during his time with *EastEnders*, told me, 'I was very proud to appear in the talent contests because, in a way, people like me had no chance of getting to the Palladium by any other way. They were for the everyman and if you had a hint of talent then yeah, it could happen, and for me it did.'

It was a very clever set-up by Butlins, profiting from the holiday bookings and media coverage of each stage during the contest. The industry liked it, too, as a feeder for new talent.

Mike added, 'Thanks to that stint at Butlins I got a chance to appear on the TV show, *The Comedians*, which was made by Johnnie Hamp – a super guy – and thanks to all that I finally landed the famous Palladium. Was I daunted by it?' He chuckled. 'Well, you muppet, of course I was, but back then I had the swagger. They get a better class of laughter maker there, you know.' Mike also revealed how, thanks to the producer and star maker Johnnie Hamp, he bypassed the famous Granada Auditions for *The Comedians*. 'Well, you see, they were running short and I was, too, of money – but that is another story. Now, the thing is, I actually had an audition over the phone for the show. Because of that he put me on TV the week after and that was it – the career and everything took off, but all of us owe him lots. I mean, Johnnie really made me a star at the Palladium and I will be forever grateful, I honestly will.'

Bobby Crush
23 March 1954 – present

Another stalwart of variety was *Opportunity Knocks!* winner Bobby Crush, famous in the UK for over forty years, primarily as a pianist but also as a songwriter, broadcaster, actor and TV presenter.

Bobby became best known after six winning appearances on TV's *Opportunity Knocks!*, receiving along the way the Variety Club of Great Britain's award for 'Best New Artiste of 1972'.

I met Bobby when he was preparing for his wonderful show based on the life of another keyboard legend, Liberace. It's an odd business, this, because we met while having a séance on stage with a medium of dubious talents trying to make contact with the late great entertainer and sadly failing. The medium claimed he could only get Michael Jackson that day but was willing to give it another go. In the meantime, Bobby began to tell me all about his career and time at his favourite theatre.

'At the tender age of eighteen,' he said, 'I found myself starring at the London Palladium, with an album in the top twenty and a single ('Borsalino') in the top forty. It was a magical time and you know when people say they were not ready and all that? Well, for me that was not the case. I loved it. Finally all my dreams were coming true and getting even better.'

Bobby went on to play three seasons at the London Palladium, guest starring with Jack Jones, Vic Damone and Dame Julie Andrews. He was thrilled when his name was then included in the famous 'Roll of Honour' at the Palladium's stage door.

'I cried when they told me that, I mean, I know I am only a small part of it but wow, like, you know – little me, outside the Palladium. I think all artistes who have their name outside should be happy; it's a wonderful thing, really, and above all else tells the world you have arrived. I won't ever lose the memories of being a young lad on that stage and sharing it with greats such as Jack Jones, who to me is a super singer, and of course Dame Julie Andrews, who looks better every time I see her. I do think it all goes so fast and you must smell the roses ,as they say. Yes, I am a Palladium kid through and though.'

Debbie Reynolds
1 April 1932 – present

Debbie Reynolds is best known for co-starring with Gene Kelly in the great Hollywood musical *Singin' in the Rain*. She was married to another Palladium favourite, the late Eddie Fisher, and of course was the mother of *Star Wars* icon Carrie Fisher.

Debbie is fabulous in real life and I have been fortunate to interview her many times in Hollywood and London. The singer and dancer, who has oodles of talent, told me of her favourite visit to London, when she came over to star in her own one woman show at the Palladium. 'I was making my debut,' she recalls, 'which is not a bad venue to make it at, right? The whole of my show was booked direct from Las Vegas and I think it was my idea to ask my daughter Carrie to come along so we could do something together. I mean, it's the Palladium, right? So I was thrilled when she agreed.

'It was the very hot summer of 1974. We opened to rave reviews and I am glad to say it went very well. Carrie only did two numbers but she got the best reviews; I remember joking with her that she had stolen the show. I was so very proud and I think, secretly, she was too. I mean, apart from Judy and Liza I think we were the only mother and daughter act to grace the Palladium stage.'

Debbie added, 'I had bought Carrie this wonderful white gown to wear on the show – well, I mean, I thought it was wonderful. She insisted on wearing black rather than the lovely white dress I'd gotten her, but I was still so proud of her.'

Had Debbie forgotten her earlier appearance at the Palladium – a duet with her husband – in the 1950s? They were photographed on stage together looking very much in love.

I showed Debbie the picture and she laughed. 'I know, it's funny how you block out things. I heard that Eddie had written a book, but who knew he could write, eh?'

Johnnie Ray
10 January 1927 – 24 February 1990

So much has been written about Johnnie Ray and his remarkable turn at the London Palladium. The footage that you see testifies to it all. He was indeed a great performer, shooting to fame with hits like 'Cry'.

I met him in the 1980s, when he was not doing as well but nonetheless had enduring star quality. He spoke of his time at the theatre, recalling great memories. 'You have to remember, this was pre-Beatles and pre-Elvis, so yeah, I think I helped create the rock 'n' roll tricks at the venue, to be honest.'

'Val Parnell was a great guy and gave me the chance to make a crack at the theatre,' he added. 'You see, he had foresight and knew that I could bring in a younger crowd, which was great for business. I will never forget it – he was a gem of a guy.'

Johnnie, like all good pop stars, fell out of favour over the years but he made a sensational comeback in 1974.

Where? At the Palladium, of course, thrilling crowds twenty years after he originally shook and wowed the house down. This was his old haunt and he was a huge success, receiving a fifteen-minute standing ovation. It was a well-deserved victory.

Johnnie told me that his later years were filled with experiences of being second fiddle. People didn't want to talk to him – they were more interested in his co-stars like Marilyn Monroe and Judy Garland. He lamented, 'The thing is with these people, I think they would find it quite funny, you know, being seen as legends and held up in such great high esteem today, because they could not have foreseen that at all during their lifetime.'

Des O'Connor
12 January 1932 – present

When you meet Des O'Connor it's like you've known him for years – always polished yet offering the ease of warm familiarity.

I was standing on the stage of the Playhouse theatre in the heart of London, waiting for my first interview with the great man. Usually I would be running through my questions, or at least a direction for chat, but I was absorbed in Playhouse history. This was the stage that hosted the BBC's radio theatre show in the 1940s and 1950s. It had welcomed so many wonderful variety acts including *The Goon Show*, *Steptoe & Son* and 'Hancock' in *Hancock's Half Hour*.

I was jolted from my daydream by the arrival of – a teddy boy? No, it was Des, dressed in character for his role in the hit musical *Dreamboats & Petticoats*.

'Playing the more seasoned part – I'm hoping to win "most promising newcomer" at the awards shows next year,' he giggled, and cheerily revealed, 'this is my first time in a musical. I always wanted to do one and the time was right; I spoke with producer Bill Kenwright who allowed me to adjust certain bits that I felt good with, like my song 'Hey Baby'. It's been such fun doing the show. I am now totally devoted to the idea of more musicals.' And who's to stop him?

Des has reached a golden era yet could easily pass for a man in his late fifties. I ask him what his secret is. 'Genes and, of course, taking good care of myself. I don't deny and I don't overindulge, that is the secret; plus I enjoy life and my career, I really do. It's been such a ride and such fun.'

Ah, the career that has seen Des as a singer, a compère, a chat show host, a game show host and a rather good egg all round. This is a guy who has topped the bill at the world famous London Palladium for weeks on end and holds records there. How nice to hear that that theatre could be the 'stage' for his golden era and long may it continue – but how did it start?

Des was keen to impart the story of his break by becoming a red coat at the Fiely camp for Billy Butlin (29 September 1899 – 12 June 1980). 'I loved it there and yes, they were great days, because you learned so much. You have to remember I was very young and more than a little gauche, so I learned how to deal and speak with people from all walks of life. Butlins was a swish operation, too, and at that time not as easy to get into as one might think. It was seen as a glamorous job, but you did everything from helping out with meals through to dancing with the more mature ladies at the famous Hawaiian ballroom. And yes, you really did have a sign saying, "Baby crying in chalet number ... " at the side of the stage, which was a novelty then, if not a tad annoying if you were the act on stage,' Des laughed.

His biggest memory was filling in for the regular guy who played a pirate in the camp. 'This meant being near the water and, of course, I said I could swim. Well, I could, but not that great, so I lived in fear of being thrown in the pool.

'Well, it happened,' Des continues. 'The little angels chased me all around the camp. My presence was announced over the tannoy. "The Pirate was now within the camp." The little blighters cornered me and were quite rough, pulling hair and kicking. I couldn't strike back; after all, they were kids. That is where I learned a lot of my craft. I have a lot to thank Butlins for, I really do.'

I wanted to ask Des his feelings on topping the bill for the first time at the Palladium. I wanted to know what it was like when Des walked up the famous Argyle Street and saw his name in high letters. His story was more than revealing.

'Ah well, for me it was a bit different, really,' Des recalls, 'as I was lucky to have a bit of an apprenticeship at the theatre before going there solo. At the time I was doing a week at Finsbury Park Empire, which was great. I got word that they were looking for someone to help out at the Palladium after an act was ill or something. I recall the night starred Harry Secombe, who was just wonderful, you know, and other really good acts. Stunned, yes, but thrilled all the same as I knew the breakthrough that this would give me.'

'What you have to remember too is that you got to watch and learn in the wings from all these greats. Alma Cogan, the girl with the giggle in her voice – Beryl Reid and of course Harry himself, who was such a kind man really and was so funny on and off stage; he was never off, as they say, in fact.'

'So for a period I was doing four shows a day, sometimes eight on matinees, as I skipped back and forth between the theatres. Did I feel exhausted? Not at all. This was the Palladium. So yes, in a way I was gently coaxed into that world and that stage, so there were not as many first time nerves as there could have been.'

Des has clocked up over 1,000 appearances at the theatre and I was keen to know how he compared each experience with a Royal Variety show. 'Ah, they were good,' he said. 'I mean, I loved doing them and we had such great stars to introduce – the list was endless. We really had the pick of the crop in those days. Nervous, of course, but I am a big fan of the royal family and I figured they must have liked the act as I was never sent to the tower! But seriously, I think it's the biggest honour for anyone to be invited to perform on that show. It's the pinnacle of your career; after all, there is no higher audience, now is there?'

Keeping his feet more or less on the floor, Des added, 'I loved doing the variety tours as well, as they were learning places. I mean, you had so much talent on one bill and you got to see so much of the country. Of course many of the famous "landladies" stories are true but as

I was so young I had no idea really; I mean, I was just busy enjoying myself. I was in showbiz doing the thing I wanted to do – entertain.'

Summer seasons played a huge part of the success of Des and he readily admits that he misses the days of twice nightly variety on a blazing hot coastline around the UK. It's when and where the great Eric Morecambe OBE (14 May, 1926–28 May, 1984) started to tease Des and his voice.

Des told me, 'They were days of innocence, really – great seasons. I mean, the work could be over sixteen weeks in one place, which was super. You also got to meet and greet many other stars. Looking back I think that's how the now famous Eric Morecambe gags about my singing started.'

'You know, people often think I was offended when he attacked me on stage and on TV but I loved it, really. I mean, it got me talked about. Old ladies would come up to me and offer sympathy and such because "that nasty Eric said some awful stuff about you last night on the TV". Little did they know that I would often supply the insult to Eric and Ernie as I knew what they could get away with!

'Eric, though, was a card. He was a total joker yet never switched off; he was always ready to entertain and I miss him dearly. Both Eric and Ernie were so talented and I admired Ernie just as much. He really did have so much talent that was not always allowed to shine because of the comedy they did, but nonetheless it's heartwarming now to think they are so well loved.'

Des landed his first big TV series in 1963 and admits that the TV bosses relied heavily on the golden age of variety for guest stars. 'Far from ruining a career, it could help; after all, you were seen by so many people and tended to get panto and a summer season out of the appearance.

'After some summer seasons doing well I recorded a hit, "I Pretend". I was doing a show in Great Yarmouth when it hit number one and to land a hit when the Beatles and the Stones were still around was great news. I never really planned a career as a pop star, it just happened. Thirty-six albums later I suppose I am doing ok,' he said, laughing.

Des, as ever the pro, returned to his first love at the Palladium playing the wizard in the spectacular Lord Lloyd-Webber production of *The Wizard of Oz*. 'It's a small part, you know,' Des said, 'but I love the fact I am here again, I just love it, and I think Lord Webber knows I would have done it for nothing if he had asked. But don't tell him that, will you?'

Standing in the number one dressing room together at the Palladium, I noted that the walls are lined with framed posters featuring all the great shows that Des has appeared in at the theatre. He jumps up to point out the variety himself. 'I loved them all. I never wanted to not go to work here. Not many people can say that, really, can they? But yes, the Palladium will always have a special place in my heart.'

Watching Des from the royal box as we film his performance for TV, it's hard to believe just how long he has been going; it's obvious from the moment he enters the stage, though, that the affection from his devoted audience is there in spades. When Des takes to the floor for the finale it really is a masterclass in how to win an audience over. They are up on their feet and totally in the palm of his hand. As ever, the last word goes to Des. 'I owe it all to variety and its inception; it really did shape the entertainer I am today. In fact I am never happier than when I am in front of an audience in a nice theatre.' The audience roars with approval and, if ever it were needed, that is the real testament.

Tony Bennett
3 August 1926 – present

Tony Bennett was born in Astoria, Queens, New York, and had his first hit, 'Because of You', in 1951. He made a career singing popular standards, including his signature song, 'I Left My Heart in San Francisco'.

Bennett's career took many twists and turns and I was hugely excited and humbled when I got the chance to interview him for international TV at the wonderful Dorchester Hotel. He was in town to launch a new album of duets, already a huge success, and to appear as a guest mentor on *X Factor*.

I had been told that Tony could be tetchy in interviews, which made me a little nervous, not least considering the scale of production involved. We had twenty of his staff waiting in and around the suite, all talking into walkie-talkies and muttering things like 'he has left his room'.

While waiting, I observed that he had chosen the suite where Dame Elizabeth Taylor had held court so many times. The Dorchester was her favourite hotel in London and perhaps this suite was reserved for the greats. Tony had the same flower designer as Taylor, too, whose job it was to strew flowers artistically over the Steinway in the corner of the room. She looked like Mrs Havisham in *Great Expectations* and watching her did nothing to quell my nerves. I took a breath; the door flew open and in walked the legend himself, Mr Tony Bennett.

We started with *X Factor* and he told me, 'You know, I like those types of shows, because they are similar to those myself and Rosemary Clooney did live on the radio every week. We did them live and we would sing lots of new songs each week. The ones they (the listeners) voted for we would play again and again, so it was like auditioning new songs for a playlist on the radio, hard work but great fun. So yes, I do admire those people because you know what? We all have to start somewhere.'

Now, back to the real core of variety and 'that' venue – the London Palladium. Tony told me that his one strong memory of the Palladium was the invitation to appear on *Sunday Night at the London Palladium* in 1958 for Val Parnell.

'This was a great show, you know,' he said, 'I mean, the biggest event on TV in the week, so for sure I am going to say yes. But truthfully I was nervous, too, it was all totally live and even though it was a tough gig in that respect, I loved it.'

Tony recalled also that the show was hosted not by Brue Forsyth but by the celebrated actor Robert Morley CBE (26 May, 1908–3 May, 1992), whom he adored. 'He was so English and beautifully spoken, which I was fascinated by as a guy from the Bronx and all that. He took time out to speak to all of us. I loved the guy. He told me he had my albums – I am really eating this up, now – but then prior to going on stage he turned to me and said, "Remind me again, what's your name?" I know he was joshing around, but you know, it was a funny thing to say.'

Tony also recalled that he appeared with another blonde bombshell that night by the name of Sabrina, who was of course Norma Sykes in real life. At the height of her fame, Norma was described as Marilyn Monroe, Diana Dors and Jayne Mansfield all rolled into one and she played this tag to the hilt. She was the main star guest on Arthur Askey's show but was never given much to say as Askey felt that her accent, which was pure Lancashire, would not be understood by the great British viewing public.

Tony had other memories of meeting Norma. 'She was very sweet and, yes, she had an amazing figure, but she wasn't as dumb as they say. She knew what she was selling. She told me that she loved being a sex symbol and asked me what contacts I had in Hollywood, as she was keen to progress her acting career beyond just standing and looking great. That was another abiding memory from doing that show.'

He added, 'You have to remember, I had had hits but 'My Heart' – my signature tune – was not out until a few years later, so Val Parnell knew that this would help me greatly and it did. Val also gave me a great piece of advice, which I have kept to, but I suppose he told all the US stars visiting the same thing. He told me, "You know, you should come to England every year, because the fans here are wonderful. If they take to you, they really take to you and you can have a career here even if no one else wants you." That is great advice and he was so right, you know. I mean, he was a brilliant man, really, looking back.'

Remember I had been warned about that 'tetchy character'? Well, don't believe a word of it. Tony was a great guy and the interview ended up being syndicated around the world. He was so pleased with it he later told me he showed it prior to his live stage performances in Las Vegas. He was also very kind, inviting me along to see him in action, and boy, what a night. After a great show and a sheer master class in musical performance, I was welcomed into the after-show party where I met more wonderful names from variety, which in turn led to many more great interviews. I have much to thank Mr Tony Bennett for.

Donny Osmond
9 December 1957 – present

Donny was just a teenager when he shot to the top as the baby face of the Osmond Brothers. The Osmond Brothers were an entertainment phenomenon, releasing hit after hit, taking the UK by storm and touring the world to thrill audiences, both young and old. It was 'Osmondmania' – fan riots and hysteria matched that for the Beatles.

Donny's debut single, 'Sweet and Innocent', became his first Top 10 hit at the age of fourteen. He later went on to release million-selling hits like 'Go Away Little Girl', 'Puppy Love' and 'Too Young'. 'Puppy Love' was his first number one hit in the UK and a smash hit worldwide.

I have been fortunate to interview all the Osmonds at various points in my career; a great pleasure, as what you see is what you get with these guys – pure charm and talent. Meeting Donny at the Grosvenor House hotel was an added bonus and he looked as young as ever.

Donny has great memories of his appearances at the London Palladium. The first time was for a US TV show called *A Royal Gala Variety Performance*. The band leader was in fact the legendary musician Jack Parnell and the producer was Bill Ward from ATV, whom Donny described as 'a great guy' who 'made it all look super'.

'I was young, so young,' Danny recalls, 'and the show had great names on it, too, so we were, like, in awe, you know? Not only we were at the London Palladium with all that history and success but then, looking at the cast list, it was Dick Martin, who was the host, and your very own Des O'Connor, then Lily Tomlin and Liza Minnelli, which was a terrific show. I mean, how it could not be?'

Donny says the theatre has been good to him and his family. 'I know all my brothers were thrilled to perform there. We did a reunion for a Royal Variety show and you know what, honestly, it was brilliant. I mean, it was just the best, because that is the true spirit of showbiz – you can keep coming back time after time. The UK fans have been brilliant.

'You see, our mentor, Andy Williams, told us great things about the theatre and its audiences, so in a way we had a sneak peak of what it's like. But nothing quite prepares you for when those curtains go back, does it?'

Russell Watson
24 November 1966 – present

Russell Watson never imagined he would someday be recognised as one of the world's greatest tenors. Yet to date, there have been over nine albums, each going into the top ten in the UK and each winning more praise than the last.

Russell popped into the studios and our conversation quickly turned to the Royal Variety show and the Palladium. He was preparing to appear at the theatre as part of his one-man show that summer and he managed to capture the feeling of 'that place' with ease. He said, 'When I was starting out, working in a dead-end factory job, I dreamed of that theatre. When it happened, it happened with knobs on and it got even better than that, because I got to sing there at the Royal Variety with the royals in attendance. It does not get much better than that.'

'Any artiste,' he added, 'that says they're not bothered about appearing at that venue, well, they may as well just quit showbiz, because the Palladium *is* showbiz, end of.'

Joe Longthorne MBE
31 Mary 1955 – present

Joe Longthorne is loved by everyone he comes into contact with and I was able to get him for a sit down chat at our TV studios for the first time in twenty years.

Joe is recognised as one of this country's finest vocalists and live performers, held in high regard by his fellow professionals and loved and adored by his fans the world over. He is one of those few select vocalists who have earned the right to be called a 'song stylist', with an instantly recognised voice and the ability to stamp his name on every song he performs to make it his own.

Joe also possesses an incredible gift for impersonations, his repertoire packed full, from his signature impression of Dame Shirley Bassey to greats such as Tony Bennett, Sir Tom Jones, Barry Manilow and Sammy Davis Jnr. He knows how to give great value for money, as you feel you have seen them all in one night.

Perhaps surprisingly, Joe is a reserved man who has overcome many personal setbacks and, as he said, 'We all have them. It's just that when you're in the spotlight people read about them and suddenly it becomes bigger than it is.'

On the day we met, Joe had just returned from Buckingham Palace where he received his MBE. Looking dapper in a suit and tie, yet typically grounded Joe, he was still in shock when he arrived at the studios. He broke the ice by telling me that he bought his gloves for the occasion at Cleveley's market and they were only £4. 'Do they look alright?'

On the subject of the Palladium, Joe said, 'The Royal show for me in 1989 was a huge event. I mean, a lad like me from Hull doing impressions and take-offs, as we called them back then. Oh yes, it was terrifying, but you're right, for a performer you have to get a slot at the Palladium. It's like a calling card – it does help.'

'I looked at the bill that day,' Joe added, 'and I mean, did you see the list? It was topped off by the Hollywood legend, Jerry Lewis, who I had taken off in my act a few years back. Well, to be on the show with him was amazing and yet there were many more.

'I remember Michael Ball, who I have always admired, and David Essex, who to me were just so professional, but the one thing I remember was being allowed to sit and watch some of the performers run through their act during the rehearsals. It was amazing, really, sitting in the stalls of the Palladium and drinking in all the atmosphere of what you had to do – live and in front of the Royals. You know, it was great, really life-changing for me.'

Modest as ever, Joe truly earned his place on that stage. He started out in a children's show for Yorkshire TV called *Junior Showtime*, which is where we first met. The show was a cross between a variety show and *X Factor*, allowing talented children the chance to appear on TV and hopefully gain some experience and success along the way. He got his big break in 1981 when he appeared on the talent show *Search For A Star* and then went on to present *The Joe Longthorne Show* from 1988 to 1991. So his climb was gradual; it was not always plain sailing.

'I had failed auditions for *Opportunity Knocks* and *New Faces* before *Search for a Star* came along,' he recalled, 'and I am thankful for the opportunity that gave me. I think you need a grounding in performance before you go on these TV talent shows. In a way, it can come way too easy and I think they are so unprepared for when they do get the big time. I did a long slog and learned how to treat an audience. They don't have that opportunity now, which can be hard, of course, when it all goes wrong.

'Variety clubs were soaring when I was starting out, and they were like college to me. They strengthen people and show them how to work. But I say, good luck to anyone who wants to try their hand at a talent show; it's not an easy thing to do but it can offer wonderful opportunities. And many have done well out of them.'

Joe returned to his memories of the Palladium and, in particular, his big night at the Royal Variety. 'It was a posh night, as well, because that year the compère was the celebrated movie star Sir John Mills. He was a lovely, truly lovely man, who took time to reassure everyone about nerves and stuff and yet he himself had the toughest job of the night.'

Joe has, of course, made many sold-out return appearances to the Palladium. 'You get such a warm response. We have filmed a few shows there and, thanks to that lovely Matcham embrace, they have all gone well. I always say when leaving the stage door, "God willing, I will be back."'

I know, too, that God willing, Joe's fans will want him back time and time again.

Darren Day
17 July 1968 – present

Darren Day is a singer, actor and writer and can also throw his voice to some great impersonations. I first met Darren when he was recording his *Summer Holiday* album with Mike Stock and Matt Aitken at the Love This Studios in London for Simon Cowell.

Darren loved to chat and kept all the crew and I in stitches with his impressions of the famous, including, of course, Sir Cliff Richard. Darren went on to great things and openly admits that his past tabloid life may have hindered his talent and future success, but now, thankfully, things are back on track and he's recording, acting and appearing in great shows across the UK once again.

Darren had the unenviable task of having to take over from pop idol Jason Donovan when Jason finished his stint at the Palladium with the hit musical *Joseph and the Amazing Technicolor Dreamcoat*.

He was just as shocked as the next critic when he got the role, as he told me. 'It was a big thing, you know. The show was *the* event in the west end at that time and all manner of names had been bandied about, far bigger than me, then, but maybe it's the cockiness of youth. You don't take it all in, really, do you? I mean, now I look back and think "wow", to headline there and have my name above the theatre – like, wow – but I suppose I was just coasting and trying to take it all in my stride.'

Darren was a smash and was hailed as a bright young new star, to which he later said, with a smile, 'I think it's fair to say I embraced it and that has been well documented.'

He then reflects on how the famous venue changed his fortunes and then led to a successful TV and recording career. 'Suddenly there was interest from people I had tried for years to get to look at me, or take notice of my work, and it was all on the back of the London Palladium. I would ring up TV bosses and say, "I am at the Palladium, why not pop down and see me in action?" And of course, having 2,000-plus people a night screaming for you and waiting at the stage door – well, if that's not enough to convince them, what is?'

'It changed my life,' Darren finishes, 'and yet, looking back, at times it was like it happened to another person, really. But I am so glad it was me.'

Denise Pearson
13 June 1968 – present

While in the group Five Star, Denise had a massive chart run of over twenty top thirty UK singles including 'System Addict', 'The Slightest Touch' and the anthem 'Rain Or Shine'. Five Star were also the youngest British group to have a number one album and the first group to achieve seven consecutive hit singles from one album in the UK.

After the band split, Denise took time out to bring up her children and focus on her own songwriting career, but thankfully she returned to do what she does best, singing and performing.

'Oh, I remember it well. You see, my dad Buster was also our manager and he was bursting with pride when we were chosen to appear at the Royal Variety show that year, from the London Palladium, no less. Oh yes, I thought he would explode with pride.'

Denise, who looks exactly the same as she did back in the eighties, added, 'The Royal Variety show was a huge event back then, with mega stars at the top of the bill and they all wanted to shine the hardest because it was the Palladium. Dad loved *Sunday Night at the London Palladium* and that, combined with meeting the queen, was all his and our dreams come true, really.'

'What I remember most was the other stars on the show. We were star struck ourselves, you know, yet people were asking for our autographs too. It was an amazing atmosphere and people came together to make a great show. The theatre, though, is nothing like you see on TV. On TV it looks huge and, while it goes up, it doesn't go back that far and for a band like ours, who had been playing arenas and things, we were amazed by just how close they all were to us.'

Denise smiled and said, 'My great pride on the night, though, is looking out and seeing a mass of women looking stunning with lovely dresses and jewels and the men in evening dress. Our ambition was to get them to interact and clap along, and they did, and so did the royals. It was an amazing experience and one we were all so grateful for. I will never forget it at all.'

Neil with Sir Bruce Forsythe. 'This place was like my second home and I owe my career to it, honestly I do. I love it and will never tire of appearing on this stage.'

Neil with Barry Humphries. 'I wanted to play my farewell tour there simply because it's the greatest variety theatre in the world.'

Neil with Engelbert Humperdinck. 'I have only acted on stage once, and that was in pantomime at the Palladium. It's not a bad thing to have on your CV, is it?'

Neil with Lee Mead. 'To appear here says it all about your career. I mean, you have made it.'

Neil with Mike Winters. 'Bernie says to the queen – I mean, *slurred* to the queen – well, do you need the tickets, then, or what?'

Neil with Debbie Reynolds. 'I love it, but my first show was, well, memorable, as my daughter decided to wear seventies fashion on stage – not a good look then or now!'

Tony Christie
25 April 1943 – present

Tony Christie is without doubt one of our best voices ever and his hits are testament to that, from 'The Avenues' and 'Allyways' through to 'Las Vegas' and 'Maria Christie'.

He was a self-taught guitarist who became a professional singer in 1964, recording singles with groups such as the Counterbeats, the Trackers and the Pen Men. By the time he signed a solo recording contract with MCA Records in 1969, he had acquired vocal mannerisms similar to those of Tom Jones; this attracted the interest of songwriters Mitch Murray and Peter Callander, who provided Christie with his first UK top thirty entry in the early 1970s.

Tony has endured through time, having enjoyed huge success in a variety of styles and musical landscapes. He was on the original concept album of the mega-selling Rice/Webber album *Evita*, which went on to be one of the biggest selling albums in the world. He then diversified again, becoming a Euro hit in Germany with a brand new style and even worked with the producers of Modern Talking, who were quite the biggest thing across Europe, if not here in the UK.

Tony tells me that when he was first asked to appear at the Palladium he thought it was a joke. 'Well, we're from Yorkshire and you do, don't you? I thought, what, is this real? And then of course it became a reality. I am sure many have told you this but you do feel as if there is something with you, there, I mean, some kind of protection. I loved it and the whole experience. But you need to do it as an act, and yes, I was nervous – good nerves, though,' he laughed.

Lew Grade and Michael Grade CBE
25 December 1906 – 13 December 1998 and 8 March 1943 – present

Lew Grade was the last of the old-time media moguls, a genuine show-business tycoon and a great showman, a sort of Louis B. Mayer of the UK and then the world. He was born in the Ukraine but moved to the UK at an early age. From humble beginnings in east London, he became the Charleston dance world champion and then gained credibility as a theatre and talent agent, but his ambitions were even bigger.

The advent of commercial television gave him the chance to bid for a franchise from the new ITV. He succeeded and then created Associated Television (ATV 1954), which pioneered popular culture, responsible for such TV hits as *Sunday Night at the London Palladium*, Robert Powell's epic portrayal of Jesus of Nazareth and bringing shows like *Thunderbirds* and *The Muppets* to British TV.

I briefly met Lew, as well as many who worked with him, and it is clear that he adored producing for the famous Palladium. Behind his trademark cigar and puff of smoke, he told me, 'You know, just go on a hunch and if you think it will work, then go with it and the rest will follow.' It didn't always work for Lew – he suffered a financial blow investing in films – but like every entrepreneur this was just part of the overall experience. His credibility remains strong in the history of variety and in the history of 'the Grade family tree'.

Lew's brother Leslie was also a theatrical agent and his nephew (Leslie's son), Michael Grade CBE, has become one of the most recognised TV executives of modern times. Michael was chairman of the BBC from 2004 to 2006 and executive chairman of ITV from 2007 to 2009. I have been lucky enough to work for Michael and I know he, too, is a big fan of the Palladium and of course his uncle.

'It was a palace of laughter,' he told me, 'with some of the greatest. I loved just being in there with rehearsals. Then of course Lew loved his TV show *Sunday Night at the London Palladium*. He was a showman through and through and knew how to cut a great deal, which helped, but the best thing, in my mind, is that he helped bring the theatre into so many homes, with some of the greatest stars ever. For that we really have to thank him because, let's face it, we are still talking about him today.'

After leaving the executive board of ITV, Michael seized the opportunity to work on a project that focussed on the Palladium. He recalls, 'It was great getting Brucie and co. back to the theatre to talk about old times and remember what made those times great. We then did a hundred years of the theatre – we were turning into a reunion home – but long after we are all gone, the theatre will still always be the "ace" variety theatre of the world.'

Lew Grade was knighted in 1969 and in 1976 was made a life peer, taking the title Lord Grade of Elstree. He died on 14 December 1998.

Liza Minnelli
12 March 1946 – present

Liza Minnelli was born on March 12 1946, in Los Angeles, California. Her mother, Judy Garland, was an elite actress and performer and occasionally included Minnelli in her performances. Her father was the wonderful film director Vincente Minnelli. With such great pedigree it is little surprise that Minnelli was able secure opportunities in the industry, but it was her own infectious attitude that earned her the stripes of a true showbiz legend.

Minnelli pursued a stage career as a teenager and performed on Broadway, but it was in the 1970s and 1980s that she hit the big time on screen, with critical acclaim for her role in movies such as *Tell Me That You Love Me, Junie Moon, Cabaret* and *Arthur*.

Meeting Liza is like meeting showbiz royalty, and she knows it, but she makes you feel at ease – and happy.

Liza sipped her tea while we sat in the glamour of the Dorchester Hotel. 'What does that theatre (the Palladium) mean to me? Everything. I mean, I grew up there and did my apprentice bit there, you know? It was showbiz, darling,' she laughed.

'When me and Mom did a show together there in the early sixties, she was so supportive and great and of course, I was a little nervous, but let me tell you, she knew I was growing. I was not a little girl anymore – in fact, maybe I could be a problem. This happens, you know – the tiger shows its claws and the mother decides that she needs to control her young. That happened between me and Mom but she was great. As she went off stage, she went off as Mom but came back as Judy Garland, the star.

'She figured that while I was good,' Liza continued, 'this was her audience and boy, they had paid to see a Judy Garland show and they were getting one. So even if I was her daughter, right there on that stage, in her theatre, she was not going to give up that easily and of course she threw everything she had into the performance.

'For me it was great, watching her up there from the wings. The Palladium saw me grow up on stage, right there with my mom, and it's something I won't ever forget. I know she loved it. It was her world at that theatre and she always got a great reception.'

Sylvester Stallone
6 July 1946 – present

The London Palladium welcomed a Hollywood legend in 2014, none other than Sylvester Stallone, for an entertaining 'Evening with …'. Hosted by Jonathan Ross, Stallone told stories and answered questions from a very enthusiastic audience. The Palladium is, of course, no stranger to this kind of event, having hosted many over the years, but I was intrigued to know what made the world's number one box office star take to the floor in such a great venue.

'You know, Neil, what I liked about the whole event was this. I have often been asked to appear and do one-man shows and this type of thing, but when this was put to me it was quite simple; they had me at the venue. Honestly, it was that simple and you know, you get such a great sense of history when you arrive. Without a doubt, it's steeped in it.'

Sylvester was a huge success at the theatre and it was something that he was choked up about as he told me, 'I hoped that people would come along and enjoy it but the reaction was super and, looking back, it was like a dream. They created this little home from home set on stage and I felt great up there. Would I come back? Like a shot,' he laughed, but added, 'as long as the theatre is the London Palladium.'

Lionel Blair
12 December 1931 – present

It seems that Lionel Blair is so famous you could be forgiven for forgetting what he is famous for. There are only a few like Lionel who have done so much for the good of the variety show business. Perhaps he is up there with Sir Bruce Forsyth.

During the 1980s Lionel was best known as the captain of the men's team on that cosiest of television parlour games, *Give Us a Clue*. It pulled in over 10 million viewers per episode and, as Lionel points out, 'We had great star guests at the time. I mean, there was Sir Bob Geldof, who loved the show, and Spike Milligan, who was a great comedy hero of mine too.'

I asked Lionel if he could spot the stars that were up for it when they came on the show. 'Oh yes, you could just tell. Many were not, so we did not have them again, but so many were and I never gossip, you see, so you won't know who I am talking about,' he laughed.

To many people, Lionel was a celebrity who danced a bit, as opposed to a celebrity dancer, but to most TV producers he was the embodiment of light entertainment, a composite of glitter, glamourous smile, awe-inspiring hair and swivelling hips. It's a role and image he relishes even to this day, adding, 'I get all the camp stuff and all that, but you know, it's showbiz, and that is what we do. If you want dull look, somewhere else. I mean, what is it with people that don't like to dress up and enjoy themselves and, well, love life?'

It's hard to shut Lionel up. Not that I wanted to, as I have waited years to get a sit-down with him and he does not disappoint at all. He is the epitome of old school charm and just such a talent.

We arranged to film an interview at the TV studios and like all good professionals he is on time, beautifully dressed and a true gent to everyone he passes, from the doorman to our makeup lady, Ann, who assures Mr Blair, 'Hardly anything needs doing.' Then he zips into the studio – and I mean zips – with the energy of a man half his age, and we're off.

Lionel is of Lithuanian decent and carried his father's name, Ogus, through his youth. His parents were working in Montreal, Canada, at the time of his birth and moved a year later to London – more precisely, Tottenham and Stamford Hill.

The Oguses were a close family. Whenever his father Myer and mother Deborah had people round to visit, Lionel (answering to his first name, Henry) and his sister Joyce (also a performer, who sadly passed away in 2006) would be the entertainment.

'It was the way for so many people, really, looking back,' said Lionel. 'I mean, it's hard for people to fathom now that entertainment was self-made, because money was tight. People got around a piano and entertained themselves, really, but it was a happy home and my parents did their best for me and Joyce. In fact, it was a wonderful time. We'd sing, we'd tap dance, we'd jitterbug.'

Later, the siblings would become a professional double act. But how did the son of a Baltic barber get bitten by the showbiz bug? Was it just his fun nurturing, or was he 'caught' by another name or act?

'When I was young I knew what I did not want to do, that was the problem, but I also knew I loved all the Fred and Ginger films. I mean, I adored them and always thought it was me up there on screen, which is madness when you think about it, but that is what you do when you're a kid, don't you?'

Lionel became a child actor, then a dancer. Of course, fame called very quickly but, as he explained, 'I am not trained at all. I just picked it up and that is why I love my best friend, the late great Sammy David Jr. He, like me, was a dancer and a Sagittarian. We just hit it off. He gave me a silver dollar inscribed with the message "To Lionel, because I dig you". I still carry it in my wallet.

'In the 1970s Sammy and his wife Altovise invited Susan (Lionel's wife) and me for a holiday at their mansion in Beverly Hills. Susan had never been to Hollywood before and was amazed at the lifestyles and just being in Hollywood. It still has that magic for us, really, because we were both kids that grew up on a film set in our minds. She was amazed at the size and extravagance of the houses. We felt as if we were on the set of a *James Bond* film. If we wanted to watch a movie, we simply pressed a button and a projector descended from the ceiling. The focal point of the sitting room was an aquarium in which a pair of piranha-like fish were swimming – it really was that glam, but it was his friendship that I admired most. He really was such a great friend, and you don't get many of those, do you?'

Lionel then, without hesitation, reminded me of a great clip of himself and Sammy at the Royal Variety show in which they sang and danced together. 'It became a cult viewing on social media,' he told me, and looking at the clip you can see why. It's professional, right down to the last tap. Both men were at the top of their game.

Lionel then began to tell me more about his favourite theatre, the London Palladium. 'The Palladium was like a second home to me in the seventies,' he enthused. 'I performed and choreographed there many times. I went back there recently and it was simply lovely, really, just going back. I stood in the auditorium of the West End's most celebrated theatre feeling that same thrill and nervous excitement that precedes a performance in front of royalty. Would I be equal to the task? As I stood on that great stage, decades' worth of fond memories washed over me. I recalled the glittering, big-budget pantos I'd also performed there. The casts were terrific – Victor Spinetti, Clive Dunn, Mollie Sugden and Windsor Davies were all booked one year for *Dick Whittington*. I mean, can you imagine that sort of cast now appearing in a theatre for that length of time? And we ran and ran because it was that popular. Looking back, I know why – it was because we all enjoyed it so much.

'A special role was written for me in the panto and I hammed up my part as the Sheriff of London for all I was worth. I was a total pro, of course; we added so much into the performance and it was one of the best stints I have ever done in a theatre. It really was that good, but we won't see the like of that again.'

He continued, 'Then there were the Royal Variety Performances. I first danced at the Palladium in the sixties. I was young and so excited just to be standing there on that stage. I mean, looking around now at your young studio staff, I don't think they can know or appreciate what it meant to us at their age to do that, but it was wonderful and I would love to step back in time to do it all again, for sure.

'Much later, I was asked to organise a line-up of American performers to commemorate the Queen Mum's eightieth birthday. Henry Mancini, Leslie Bricusse, Mary Martin and her son Larry Hagman were among the stars I invited. Larry was a huge star at the time, thanks to his TV shows like *I Dream of Genie* and, of course, *Dallas*, in which he played the big bad oil baron J. R. Ewing, so to get him involved was a real coup and people were super excited that he was on the show.

'I can still recall how nervous Larry got as he tried, during rehearsals, to remember the list in "My Favourite Things", that classic song from *The Sound of Music*, which he was to sing in front of the Queen Mum. The harder he tried the more tongue-tied he became. In a way, we all felt for him and did wonder just how he was going to get on that night. I mean, bad enough doing it to an ordinary audience, but then in front of the Queen Mum too!'

So what happened to poor old Larry? Lionel chuckled. 'Well, on the night of the live performance he was struck by stage fright and, sure enough, he fluffed his lines but he kept going. I think, as he told me after, he was dying inside but like all good showbiz stories it was that old trouper, his mother Mary, who swept out of the wings and saved his skin. She was then approaching seventy, but she got such a burst of adrenaline from stepping into the spotlight that she looked and performed like a woman half her age. As she sang and danced to a rapt audience, she was a young woman again and I recall thinking I'd be delighted if I could hoof it like her when I reached her age.'

Lionel can certainly still dance and, as he told me, 'I loved the Palladium with all my heart. I mean, I would still like to take my one-man show there because, in a way, you know that the theatre will save you. Very few have said that they didn't enjoy their time at that theatre.

'I look at it occasionally,' he added, 'and just dream away. If I go to a show I am lost in thought prior to the curtain going up and stuff. It just has so many wonderful memories for me.'

Roy Walker
31 July 1940 – present

It is almost twenty years since Irish comedian Roy Walker left our television screens after a fourteen-year stint as the presenter of the Saturday night game show *Catchphrase*. Fittingly, it was his 'say what you see' slogan and cheesy humour that made him a household name.

Roy carries his humour on and off the stage and, having met him quite a few times now, it's always a pleasure to sit down and have a chat. One such time was at the famous

North Pier Theatre in Blackpool where Roy always had the audiences howling with laughter. He was cleverly clean with his jokes, which captured the funny side of life. The best bit is that we could all relate to them.

Roy recalls his big TV break in the 1970s when he appeared on the now almost forgotten talent show *New Faces*. It was yesteryears' equivalent of today's *X Factor*, but without the phone voting. Originally presented by Derek Hobson, *New Faces* was produced by ATV for the ITV network. The first pilot was shown on 7 July 1973 and then a full series from September 1973 to April 1978. It was recorded at the ATV Centre in Birmingham and was a great platform for many future stars, including Les Dennis, Gary Wilmot and Victoria Wood.

The biggest fascination of the show, though, was the panel, which featured greats such as record producer Mickie Most – the one-man hit machine in the seventies who was straight but fair with the acts, prominent comedian and actor Arthur Askey who was always sympathetic and encouraging and Tony Hatch – the composer, singer and soap theme-tune icon who was renowned for his less-than-kind but very honest comments. It was Tony who many believe had a great influence on Simon Cowell.

When Roy appeared in 1977, he received the highest marks ever given to a comedian and, of course, he has since gone on to great success; as he recalls, however, the early days were tough. 'I did all my training in Scotland when I was a young comic doing working men's clubs. I love a Scottish audience, they love to laugh.'

However, the nation was not always as hungry for Walker's wit. It took time to win over a wider audience and, like most comics starting out on the circuit, he struggled for a while. 'Oh yes,' he said, 'I had some bad nights, and I mean bad nights, but looking back I always think you need it, in a way, because what you're doing is trying to get people to like you and your humour. There is no guarantee of that and why should there be?'

After winning *New Faces*, Roy went on to many TV slots, including a stint for producer Johnnie Hamp on the hit TV show *The Comedians*. 'That was a great show but tough, you know, because you had all these comics together and of course we had Bernard Manning. Bernard was nice off stage and a great bloke, but yes, there was a bit of rivalry on stage because it's all about being quick, and all that. Plus Bernard was the star of the show and I knew it and we all knew it, because he told you. That was the funny thing about Bernard.'

I asked Roy about his Palladium experience. 'Well, Neil, I am fortunate enough to be able to say that I have been there many times now and as a comic, you know you have made it without a doubt. Well, you have unless you bomb there, of course,' he laughed.

'One big event I do remember was a TV show made by LWT at the time, a no-expense-spared Christmas show, which had Johnny Mathis at the top of the bill. They created a Victorian snow scene outside the theatre and it even had carol singers and all that. I mean, can you imagine that now, really? The expense alone – it would not happen.'

'The show was called *A Night of One Hundred Stars*, a huge event, and really, being on that show and in that theatre I felt, well yes, my boy, you have arrived. We were all backstage, looking at who was who, from Moria Anderson through to Elaine Stritch and people like the late great Martin Caine. So we have the likes of me with Norman Collier, another great comic and so wonderful and warm, plus people like Joe Longthorne and Sue Pollard mixing with such greats. It was an explosive night and really went well. We were all so excited just to be involved. I don't think you will see the likes of that style of entertainment again and the Palladium was just glorious.'

When he is not performing stand-up, or penning his memoirs, the veteran television star is cruising about on his Triumph Thunderbird motorbike. He also enjoys keeping fit – he is a former Northern Ireland hammer-throwing champion – and visits the gym three times a week.

Roy has no plans to retire; he is ready for whatever life throws at him and hasn't ruled out a return to television.

'I am a great believer in fate. If it's for you, you'll get it,' he said. 'You have to think that way or else you won't really become the person you should be – that is what I think, anyway. When I was forty-four, I got my first television series and I stayed on prime-time television on Saturday nights for fourteen years, so I think I am worthy of another job. My ambition would be to get another game show. I do think the game shows are far too intricate, now, and need to be a lot more basic – like a parlour game show, really allowing the whole family to get involved again.

'I haven't seen a show that I'd like to present, because *Catchphrase* is still so popular with every age group. I think it was a premature decision to take it off and yes, it's back, but how about me doing a daytime version for the older viewers who watched it the first time around? It could be a great success.' And with that, he strolls into the stage door of the North Pier theatre for another roaring night of laughter and appreciation.

Bernard Manning
13 August 1930 – 18 June 2007

Bernard Manning has been called many things in his time and thankfully, this includes 'funny'.

By the age of twenty, Manning had started earning extra money singing in local clubs. This led to a variety theatre engagement at the Manchester Palace, where he was billed as 'Britain's newest singing thrill'.

After a few months of singing for Oscar Rabin's band in London, he left Rabin and moved back to Manchester, where he got a job as the resident compère at the Northern Sporting Club. Slowly, he began to introduce comic patter between the songs and, as the jokes received a better response than the tunes, he morphed into a stand-up comedian. He was successful and, moreover, he had the confidence and entrepreneurial spirit to keep growing. He especially liked the idea of an impresario and decided to buy the Temperance Billiard Hall in Harpurhey, converting it into the Embassy Club, which opened in December 1959. He thrived more or less for the rest of his life.

A decidedly family business, it was set up with money lent to him by his father, and staffed by his parents and some of his siblings. Manning compèred the shows and Jimmy Tarbuck, Matt Monro and the Beatles were among the acts he introduced. Much later, his only child Bernard took over the management of the club.

Meeting Bernard Manning is of course a terrifying prospect, but he is a kind gentleman, making you feel welcome and at ease. Within minutes, he tells me of his own Palladium experience. 'You know with our show *The Comedians*, well, we were booked into the first season for about two weeks, nothing more, and we were also told that while the TV show was a success and the Blackpool season had been a sell-out, we should not expect the same in London.'

Bernard continued, 'The thing is, laughter is laughter and as I said to our producer John Hamp, it's all that matters. But yes, doing the Palladium was a big event, not just for me but for all of us. I mean I have to say it was not the best welcome, not really – it was one of those things. You got the impression that people thought we would fail and of course the London critics are not going to be kind, now are they?

'We had a great team, of course – Mike Reid, Charlie Williams, who they said was too broad with his Yorkshire accent, and then Ken Goodwin, who was so happy to be at the Palladium. I mean, we all were, really, but unlike the other boys I had a successful club and felt that while it was a great venue I was not on stage at my own club every night, so yeah, that is what was going through my mind.'

With a smile, Bernard added, 'The upshot of it all was that we were a smash, and I mean a smash. We ended up staying at the theatre for five months, yet many people could not believe why we were so successful. But it's as I have always said – if it's funny, it's funny, and that is all that counts. I think it shocked everybody, including us. The best bit was seeing our names outside the theatre. That is when it got me. I mean, I never thought in a million years I would see my name outside the famous London Palladium. We all used to stand on the stage and just look out, because you have to remember, all of us from *The Comedians* had come from a poor background; we all stood there looking at that vast Matcham building wondering just how we landed there.'

The show was so popular it was extended over the summer season and was completely sold out.

Bernard returned to the Palladium on numerous occasions and told me, 'It's simple; the audiences in the London Palladium are no different to the audiences in my club up here in Manchester. They want, no, they need laughter and that is what we gave them. If you make people laugh, yes, the venue might be posher, but it's all the same when it comes down to the act.'

Meeting Bernard was an experience. He shed his own sort of light on the great Palladium. Sadly, he passed away in 2007 but just before our last chat, he told me he had a secret meeting and would fill me in later. It turned out that pop queen Madonna had booked him as a special treat for her then-husband, film director Guy Ritchie, as he was, apparently, 'a huge fan'. Bernard told me afterwards, 'She was great and totally got all the jokes and joined in the fun. They said I would never make it in the US but it appears that she got it, so why would no one else?'

Bernard also performed in front all of major royals, including Prince Charles, who admitted to me, 'Bernard can be terribly naughty, but then, it's fun and he does not mean any harm. He just enjoys seeing people enjoying themselves and that's a nice thing, don't you think?' Victoria and David Beckham were also fans.

So what were Bernard's highlights? In his own words, 'My own club, appearing in Las Vegas and starring at and filling the London Palladium. I knew that once I had done that I could die happy.'

Bernard Delfont
5 September 1909 – 28 July 1994

Boy, what a showman and what an impresario – Baron Bernard Delfont, the eighty-four-year-old doyen of the Grade family, who dominated post-war British entertainment. His showbiz siblings, Leslie and Lew, earned many a nod of approval but Bernard was simply fabulous, not just for his immaculate blow-waved hair but for his unrivalled ability to spot a hit show and his being in charge of the Palladium for over twenty years.

After leaving school at twelve, Bernard became a professional dancer, taking the stage name Delfont. He later became a theatrical agent before he moved into staging shows. During the Second World War, he bought up cheap leases on West End theatres – he was no fool.

I was in the glitzy entertainment capital of Blackpool when I met this showbiz legend – a case of being in the right place at the right time. He was presenting his long-running, star-studded summer show at the North Pier. I was a young kid hooked on the industry and he took the time to show me around his beloved pier.

We sat down for a cup of tea and it seemed natural that the conversation moved quickly to his favourite topic – himself – and, in particular, his time as the boss of the biggest show in the world, the Royal Variety Performance.

Bernard was the producer of the Royal Variety for twenty-one years (1958 – 1978 inclusive) and life president of the actors' charity, the Entertainment Artistes Association. He was involved with many other show-business charities, describing himself as 'an impresario of pleasure'; that is what he set out to do, and he did so successfully.

'Hopefully people will see it like that when I am gone,' he said.

Bernard was impressed that I had read his book, because he told me, 'I figure I don't appeal to young people but it's nice if they do enjoy it.'

Bernard then explained how he became successful. 'It's all down to hard work, really, and being able to pick and execute a successful show. It's not just the stars that you have to think about but the whole show. You then sit back and think, will this appeal to the masses? And if you can mix it up well then yes, you have a successful show.'

Mr Delfont insisted I called him Bernard, or Bernie, but you got the impression that he much preferred to have people know who he was and have the respect he was due. This was a man who took charge of the greatest variety show on earth and staged it with flair, time and time again, at the greatest variety venue, the Palladium. Bernie is nice, but Mr Delfont seemed more appropriate.

'You see,' he said, 'with the Royal Variety show, its natural home is the London Palladium and that is what makes the big US stars want to come over and appear on the show for free. It's the lure of the theatre and they know all those names that have gone before them. It's the perfect way of asking whoever is huge at that time to make the journey. "It's at the Palladium," and then the icing on the cake, of course, "in front of our beloved British Royal Family." Only one star refused the opportunity in my time.'

Who, who? I pushed, but he refused to tell me. Even so, my money is on Barbara Streisand, who was in London during 1965 and starring in Delfont's production of the Broadway smash *Funny Girl*. He let slip that, while he was in awe of her talent, he was less than impressed with the fact she agreed to such a short run of the show. It transpired, 'She was expecting her first child at that time but never bothered to let me know.'

Bernard also told me one of his favourite comics was the late great Jack Benny. 'I booked Jack Benny for the royal show, as I heard that the queen and duke were fans, and boy, what a great idea. I could see them crying with laughter and I mean that seriously. That is what I mean about being someone who brings joy to people. That is what makes me happy.'

The last time I saw Mr Delfont was at the launch of yet another great idea that he dreamed up. He noticed that people of a certain age were finding it harder to get down the pier – primarily to see his shows, of course – so he installed a new tram to take the guests down. Being a 'Delfont idea' he decided to do it in style, bringing the famous car of *Chitty Chitty Bang Bang* to the launch. A showman to the end.

He told me why the theatre and Blackpool were so special to him. 'People tell me there is a north–south divide, but not with my shows, because if it's good, it's good. If a show sells out at the Opera House or here at the North Pier, chances are it will sell out at the Palladium, because you're giving people style and class and that is a great thing.'

I go to Blackpool often and see the now-disused tram track. Of course, there is talk of it coming back, but while they decide if they can afford the renovations it remains rusting and empty. Often, while walking along the pier, I recall the hot, sunny day when the king of showbiz, Lord Delfont, was so happy, with his bouffant hair blowing in the North Sea breeze as he watched all the people boarding his tram to take his customers down to enjoy his latest spectacular. You just can't help but smile, because that is what he did for so many people, not just at the Royal Variety shows but around the UK where, as he insisted, 'You're never far from a Delfont spectacular.'

Simon Webbe
30 March 1978 – present

Simon Webbe is an English singer-songwriter, actor and manager. He is perhaps best known as a member of the British boy band Blue. The band released their debut single, 'All Rise', in May 2001 and it reached number four in the UK singles chart.

The Palladium has many fans from among the rich and famous, and also from those of the younger generation. This included Simon, when Blue first made the headlines. He told me in an interview that he could not quite believe his luck when he was offered a chance to appear at the famous venue in a smash hit musical, *Sister Act*, along with a stunning cast of dream artistes.

However, he explained, 'When I was first asked to do *Sister Act*, my answer was the same as I first gave to *I'm a Celebrity Get Me Out of Here*. I said "no" because of the fear factor. It's easy in a band, in a way, because half the time the fans are screaming your name and then of course there are others up there with you and you can deflect on that and move away, but this was a whole new area for me. I hadn't done stage work since I was fifteen, in school, and you're cocky then; I mean, you think you know it all.'

'The real deciding factor for me was the show itself, which was already a huge smash, along with the real opportunity to appear nightly in that theatre. You don't get it until your name is up there and you're doing it, but each night I would go in the stage door and reflect, you know, think of all those who have gone before me.

I owe my co-star in the show, Shelia Hancock, for that. Seriously, she was a huge help and made me think more about what it was I was doing and how much I would be learning. Nothing, and I mean nothing, compares to that moment when the curtain goes up and you look at the auditorium and think, "Wow, I made it." I am truly grateful for the opportunity to have appeared there. It was simply a career highlight.'

David Essex
23 July 1947 – present

David Essex was born in Plaistow, England, an only son. His father was an East End dock worker and his mother a self-taught pianist and the daughter of Irish tinkers.

David shot to fame via hit songs like 'Rock On' and 'Hold Me Close' and he remains one of the most beloved singers in the UK and beyond. I could understand why when I met him – he is talented, charming and ever appreciative of opportunities, not least appearing at the Palladium.

'Actually,' David said, 'people assume that I arrived at the Palladium already a star, because while it remains one of my favourite venues to visit on tour I do have a history with the theatre.'

'When I started out I was a jobbing actor, not a pop star at all, but it was all good fun and, of course, it was the life that I wanted to lead. Anyway, way back in 1969 I was cast as an understudy for the wonderful Palladium panto that year, *Dick Whittington*. It was lavish, quite one of the best productions I had been in to date, plus the cast were wonderful. We had the chart star Mary Hopkin, who was beautiful and had a wonderful voice, and who could forget the talent-dynamo of the late great Billy Dainty, who brought the house down night after night with his routines. I mean, we were all crying with laughter, the cast, the crew and the audience – it was wonderful.'

David went on, 'We also had the *Carry On* legend Kenneth Connor, who was as funny off stage as he was on it, but my great memory was standing in on occasion for our star and Palladium legend Tommy Steele. He was a huge star, of course, and had such expertise in how to look after an audience. I was lucky enough to step in and star in a Palladium panto, so that is why the place holds such dear memories for me. Whenever I return, it's been great. The fans and the atmosphere are wonderful. I won't ever stop appearing there.'

Jim Dale MBE
15 August 1935 – present

Jim Dale began his career as a stand-up comic. He sharpened his comedy skills during a stint in the army, where he arranged and performed in camp shows, which became a huge success. This inspired Jim to do more and more. After his discharge from the forces, he landed a job as the warm-up comic on a musical variety show. He did so well that the producers gave him a spot on the show as a singer; he quickly became a recording star. He was barely out of his teens.

At the age of twenty-two, he became the first recording artiste under the wing of the now legendary Beatles' recording manager, Sir George Martin, who produced many hit records for him over the next two years. Jim first appeared in and then hosted the two top music shows on British television, *Six-Five Special* and *Thank Your Lucky Stars*.

It was extraordinary that I ended up in the number one dressing room at the Palladium to spend over three hours with Jim Dale, who was busy starring in the production of Sir Cameron Mackintosh's hit musical *Oliver!*. Jim, who was into his fifties by this point but looked no more than forty up close, was excellent company and, for a younger writer like me, simply gold; he was generous in telling me about his career.

I arrived at the stage door but before I could take breath, Jim slid through beside me and introduced himself. I could tell he was extremely popular with the team on the show, because everyone smiled when they saw him; they all had time for a chat with him and asked how his weekend had been. I was just a tad star-struck. After all, this was Jim Dale, the man who had floated at breakneck speed on a gurney in those oh-so-famous *Carry On* films. I had seen him do everything and I was a huge fan of his work, which was extensive.

Jim took me directly on to the centre of the stage, yes, that Palladium stage, and told me, 'Now, simply stand there.' Then he had the lighting team flick on all the lights and said, 'Drink it in – this is showbiz.' He was right, of course.

After that treat, Jim organised some drinks and suggested we retire to his dressing room for the interview. As we passed along the corridors of the theatre he pointed out all sorts of things that were fascinating and of such interest I could barely take them all in.

His phone rang and this gave me a short chance to take stock. Jim had been away in the US, where he is also hugely respected as an entertainer even to this day. In fact, you could say he is something of a mega star, with the skill to reinvent himself or his character time after time. You could also see he was thrilled to be back in the UK, breaking box office records with his stint as the old rascal Fagin in *Oliver!*, and that's how we started the conversation. Our backdrop was the wonderful Fagin costume hanging in the corner.

'You know, I can become him in an instant,' he said and he did, frightening the life out of me. He oozed acting ability.

Jim explained that the show was a great production to be in, but added, 'This place – I mean, they called me over and asked if I wanted to appear at the Palladium and, as much as I love the role of Fagin and *Oliver!*, I knew it would be a success for me here. It's always been good for me here – it's not let me down yet.'

Jim recalled also how the Palladium had helped reinvent him when he became the host of the famous *Sunday Night* shows. 'I did the show in the early 1970s and, yes, you look at them now and think they are a bit cheesy, but they decided to get rid of the famous game show *Beat the Clock* and it was for more of a fair game, really, called *Anything You Can Do*.

'I thoroughly enjoyed my time here and of course I have done many other shows at the Palladium. It helped my US career no end, appearing here, because – and I am sure many others will tell you this – the theatre is the star, so if you're trying to get going in the USA and you say you have appeared at the Palladium then it's almost an open door and I am ever so grateful for that, without a doubt.'

Jim then tells me about his pop star years. 'I worked with George Martin prior to the Beatles. We had quite a few hits, actually,' and then there was his hugely successful film career and his song writing skills – so it went on. It was like variety ran through his blood.

Jim Dale is a star but also an extremely kind, generous man. I shall be forever grateful for that opportunity. The one thing that I find mystifying is that so little is written or seen about him now, here in the UK, and I believe we are far poorer for that.

Eric Sykes CBE
4 May 1923 – 4 July 2012

Eric Sykes was born in Oldham, Lancashire, the son of a millworker and former army sergeant. His mother died while giving birth to him and his father remarried a year later. He loved his school days, where he excelled at art. However, his family could not afford to send him to college, so he became a store keeper in a cotton mill. 'I actually quite liked the job, looking back,' he said. 'It was a tranquil life back then, but we had no idea, did we?'

Eric joined the Royal Air Force during the Second World War, qualifying as a wireless operator with the rank of Leading Aircraftman. The RAF asked if anyone had any theatrical experience for the entertainment shows and Eric was quick to volunteer. 'I thought, well, I've been to the theatre three times before the war, so it's as good as,' he chuckled. And he shone.

Always modest, Sykes maintained he had bluffed his way into those wartime shows. Maybe so, but he also delivered time after time and in many ways for the RAF and for his country.

After the Second World War, he decided to make his living writing comic scripts, which he told me frightened his family. 'Well, they said, that's all very well, Eric, but are you really that funny?'

His first break came when he managed to sell one of his scripts to Frankie Howard for £10. Before long he was writing regularly for radio, then for TV and film. Quite simply, he shot to fame.

Sykes was a comedy legend and I would often see him walking down to his office near where I lived in Bayswater. Meeting him for real was another stroke of luck, being in the right place at the right time again for his last ever West End show – a restoration comedy at the Piccadilly Theatre.

Like many comedy greats, Eric echoed a respect for the wonderful London Palladium. 'Of course, the Palladium was the Mecca of comedy,' he said. 'I used to go there right up in the gods and watch them all – Trinder, Miller, the big US stars and so many more, because you could learn from them and try and make it yourself.'

Eric told me that the highlight of his Palladium life was his first big panto script, *Cinderella*, in 1953, co-starring with Julie Andrews as 'Cinders'.

'The cast were fabulous and Julie Andrews, you know – she knew some jokes, oh yes. She was not always that squeaky clean,' he said with a wink. But he told me seriously, 'It was a lavish and huge production, as they were back then, and honestly, at that point I had no desire to perform except in that theatre. I saw the likes of Max and Mr Pastry (Richard Hearne) and thought I loved the sound of that applause, so yes, that was a turning point and back then we ran for weeks and weeks at a time. It was a great period for the theatre, plus there was no snobbery like there is now with panto – it was a good thing to be associated with.'

In 1954 Eric teamed up with Spike Milligan to write the script for *Mother Goose*, another hit panto at the Palladium. He later took part in a show at the theatre, titled *Large as Life*, with his close pal, the supreme actress Hattie Jacques. The two were a hit and became a TV couple loved by many. Speaking about the show, he said, 'It was super fun because we had the likes of Harry Worth, who was such a funny man and so down to earth with it all, plus Adele Leigh and Harry Secombe. I adored Harry, as we all did.'

The show was put together by Val Parnell and co-produced by Bernard Delfont. Eric described Val as 'the boss of the theatre – oh yes, a huge man, with a directness that could sting quite badly, really'. I think he was fonder of Bernard. 'He was Superman, always lovely and well turned out. I remember so many afternoons sat in each other's dressing rooms backstage at the Palladium, chewing the fat, laughing and laughing and basically all being paid to make others laugh.'

So what does it all mean to you, Eric? 'It's the best job in the world, is showbiz, and even better if you get a chance to ply your wares at the Palladium. I had my fair share of happiness and success there.'

Not long after our last meeting, Eric Sykes passed away, but what a great legacy of work he leaves behind. We all miss him and I think we always will. Eric was awarded an OBE in 1986 and the James Carreras Award for Lifetime Achievement from the Variety Club of Great Britain in 2002.

Frank Randle
30 January 1901 – 7 July 1957

Arthur McIlroy, better known as Frank Randle, was one of the top northern comics in the 1940s and early 1950s, with regular summer seasons doing variety. He made many films of dubious production quality; these were, however, financially profitable and the public lapped them up. Frank basically adlibbed and did his stage act in most of them, with only a loose script to hand.

It seemed that he had it all but, as with so many comedians, behind the laughter Randle was and remained tormented. Many blame this on his desire to achieve national stardom; while he was quite popular down south, he never attained the cult following achieved in his native north. He had numerous opportunities to do so but it wasn't to be.

Although billing himself as the world's greatest comedian, he always played second fiddle to fellow Lancastrians George Formby and Gracie Fields. Frank, though, was a one-off and this particular section of the book is courtesy of Philip Thompson and Alan Thompson, who were both lucky to have met Frank many times and witnessed first-hand his ability to pack houses on the Central Pier in Blackpool.

Dad told me of meeting the great Frank on the pier at Blackpool because, as ever, Frank had had a fall out with his musicians and my grandfather was a pianist – a brilliant one, actually – and Frank was keen to lure my grandfather to play for him at his own show on the Central Pier. Dad told me, 'The thing I remember about him was how immaculate he was in dress and how very quietly spoken. Brilliant with children and not at all the character you saw up on stage, who would belch and pass wind, which got the audience on its feet and howling with laughter.' Dad added, 'Your grandfather never did play for him, in the end, as the simple fact was that Frank was erratic. They did become friends, though, and that was how I know of his Palladium failure.'

Dad told me that they met up with Frank, not long after he came back from London after his debut at the Adelphi theatre, and I recall him not being happy at all with the show that Jack Hylton had put together. It was, I believe, like cine variety, which was no good to someone like Randle.

Dad also remembers one day, not too long before Frank passed away, when he and his father were staying at the Imperial Hotel in Blackpool and Frank just coming in for a morning cup of coffee, looking dapper as ever but in a reflective mood.

He spoke of Val Parnell and how he had hoped to get another date at the Palladium, to prove to people that he would go down well at the famous venue and that he did have an audience down there, but it appears that nothing came of it and Mr Parnell was refusing to take his calls. Dad, who was a great fan, told me, ' You could see in his eyes that he really wanted to appear there. After all, it was the big one for him in terms of showbiz; he knew that by doing that he could reinvent himself and move towards character acting, which is something he also spoke about that morning in the Imperial.'

Sadly, it was never to happen, as Frank by this time was very ill and while he was still taking his own show, *Scandals*, around, theatres were less than keen to have him now, due to his 'trouble' – or his reputation. Frank was ever the optimist, though, and told his team that 'We will crack the Palladium yet. Don't worry, it will happen.'

Frank died in Blackpool of gastroenteritis in 1957 and is buried in Carleton Cemetery, Blackpool. His memory lives on, though, as he has a blue plaque on the North Pier in the town, unveiled by former co-stars and fans, which depicts him in his most famous character, the Old Hiker. As Dad told me, 'Frank would be stunned by that, truly stunned – but yes, no doubt rising a pint to himself, too.'

Elaine Paige OBE
5 March 1948 – present

She is our very own singing superstar, a pocket dynamite of talent and a voice – oh goodness, that voice – that can evoke so many emotions. Boy, she can sing.

Reading Elaine's credits is like a history of the post-war musical. She was the first to play the iconic roles of Eva Peron in *Evita*, Grizabella in *Cats* and Florence in *Chess*. Her smash hit tunes include 'Don't Cry for Me, Argentina', 'Memory' and 'I Know Him So Well', her chart-topping duet with Barbara Dickson. Lord Lloyd-Webber regards her recording of 'As If We Never Said Goodbye', from *Sunset Boulevard*, as probably the best performance of any one of his songs. 'It's simply wonderful. Elaine brings out such character within the song,' he said.

Evita made Elaine a star, but she admitted to me that she was on the verge of quitting. 'I was fed up with the whole thing. I couldn't get the parts I wanted. I couldn't afford new clothes, I had holes in my boots, and I couldn't go out to eat. I was coming up to twenty-nine and thought I wasn't good enough. *Evita* saved me, and I mean saved me, as I have no idea where I would be now without it.'

'The funny thing is that now, of course, they find that kind of star or actress via a reality TV show, but for me I was up there alone and thrown to the lions in terms of media. It was great fun, though, and I owe it so much, I really do.'

Almost within a blink of an eye, she became a household name. She released a solo album, *Sitting*

Pretty, and received countless invitations to appear on TV. She was a regular guest singer on *The Two Ronnies* and then a total smash with audiences when she took lead roles in the musicals *Cats* and *Chess*.

At the turn of the 1990s her popularity softened, at least among producers and casting agents, and it was harder to secure roles she could make her own. Undeterred, she joined existing shows, such as *Piaf* and *Sunset Boulevard*, to equal acclaim. 'I am not at all a diva, or whatever the term is. I mean, I loved the roles that were offered and figured I would be stupid to turn them down, so I embraced them and we (with the cast) turned the shows into great successes. We had a ball. Many people forget that it's a team effort.'

Elaine has proved her worth because she has since returned to acting, too, and laughs out loud when I tell her I remember her stint on the ill-fated soap opera *Crossroads*.

'Oh, do you? Actually the show has cult fans and I was thrilled to be in it at the time, but it was always considered second fiddle to the big soaps back then. I love to act, though, and still do. It's a passion.'

Having spent time with Elaine as she glides through interviews, into TV studios or across a red carpet, I was naturally intrigued to find out what made the Palladium special for her. She was swift to answer, without a mention of her own shows.

'Oh, *The King And I*. It was a magical show to do and you know, appearing nightly in those wings waiting to go on, you do get a sense of thrill about who has been right there in that spot feeling all the nerves that you have right at that moment. I never got over that and we got a great warm reception.'

The King and I became one of the most successful musicals at the London Palladium, taking well in excess of £7 million at the box office. This was against headlines that suggested musical theatre was pretty much dead in the water.

'It took that show,' she said, 'to make sure I got my name in lights at the Palladium. You see, I had appeared in almost all the theatres in London and yes, I had sung at the Palladium in Royal Variety shows and stuff, but then, once you're the leading lady, well, things begin to look up, don't they? And it's this place.'

Elaine, though, like all good divas – or she may prefer simply 'stars' – manages to neatly forget her first appearance on that stage. With a bit of gentle research it appears that Elaine took a role in *Babes in the Wood* in 1965, which starred the legends that are Frank Ifield, Arthur Askey, Sid James, Kenneth Connor and Roy Kinnear. The production was a huge success as Frank Ifield – famous, of course, for his yodels on records – was a big hit and a teen idol to boot, so what better time to grace the famous stage?

Nudging her memory with a smile, Elaine recalled, 'Oh yes, we were part of the ensemble – Aida Foster Children, which was a dancing troupe that I was part of and what a great experience it was, for sure. I adored being in panto because as we were so young we were well looked after and I do remember the kindness of the stars like Arthur Askey, who always made us children laugh with his antics. Sid James also had us laughing and of course,

Frank Ifield, who seemed like a pop god back then. He was so tall and for a child he had some magic stardust about him.'

She wouldn't have known back then, but Elaine shared the stage with another diva-to-be – Sharon Arden, as she was then, who would later find fame as the wife of rock star Ozzy Osbourne.

Kylie Minogue OBE
28 May 1968 – present

Kylie Minogue is the eldest of three children. Her acting career began early, but it was the role of Charlene in Australian soap *Neighbours* (1985) that established the wonderful Kylie as an international star.

It took time and a magic touch for *Neighbours* to capture a UK audience. It was BBC boss and Palladium favourite Michael Grade who changed it all around and he told me, 'What we did was show it at lunch time and then repeated it in the early evening, when kids had come home from school. She (Kylie) was the perfect mix at that time. Teens adored her and we had a smash hit show every evening on BBC TV.'

Kylie's popularity made her attractive to many agents and producers, but her singing career was something of a fortunate accident when a record company executive heard her rendition of Little Eva's 1962 hit, 'The Loco-Motion'.

She remembered, 'It was for a benefit event and really, I had no intention of becoming a pop star, I mean, we all dream of it, but not seriously for me. I thought I would become an actress full time – well, I hoped I would.'

After the success of the record in Australia with Mushroom Records, she came to London and in 1987 signed with PWL Records and hit-makers, producers and songwriters Stock Aitken Waterman. Five albums and a 'greatest hits' compilation followed and she made history by having more than twenty consecutive top ten hits in the UK. She left PWL Records in 1992.

Kylie, however, admitted to me that her first Palladium appearance – the Royal Variety show in 1988 – was a blur at that time. 'It was a huge event, I mean, my parents and family could not quite believe it, really, and neither could I. We knew it was the biggest thing.'

Kylie was in good company that year, with Mickey Rooney, Ann Miller, Brian Conley and Bruce Forsyth also appearing in the show. She recalled, 'These were huge names to be associated with, but I was also very lucky on that show because my producers were having so much success with artistes that I had people like Bananarama and Rick Astley who were also with my label, PWL, so I did feel some kinship with them and we stuck together a bit.'

Kylie added, 'The event, as I say, was huge, but it was also an honour because the place – the venue – is the star, and here was I getting to sing and dance in front of the royals. I performed my song to a backing track, as the orchestra were gearing up for the next act, but I was not at all worried about singing. I was a bit nervous about having to speak in the middle and introduce my next song, "Made in Heaven". That's when a thousand thoughts go around your mind.

'It went well, but then I had to discard this jacket attire and reveal the dress. In my mind's eye, being a worrying type of person, I could see it not coming off. Thankfully it did, and my first show at the Palladium was all right, actually. I was over the moon with it.'

Kylie is a royal favourite and has returned to the Palladium many times since then, usually to a favourable media buzz and huge acclaim, but there was one 'storm' cooked up by the headline hunters. Rumours abounded that Kylie, now a bona fide pop star, was no longer associating herself with her former co-stars from *Neighbours*.

Kylie finished her song and announced, 'I would now like you to meet some good pals of mine, the cast of *Neighbours*,' and then she shot off. The press claimed that Kylie had 'snubbed them on the world famous Palladium stage', but even her former colleagues would quickly refute this unfriendly gossip. Anne Charleston, who played Kylie's mum Madge in the series, told me, 'It was agreed she had left the show and we did our bit. There was no feud at all, trust me, we all got on fine. I remember standing backstage, listening to her and thinking how well she had done in such a short time; you know, it was thanks to Kylie that we all got to stand and appear on the Palladium stage, too, so it was rather cruel of the press to make that up, to be honest.'

Fiona Fullerton
10 October 1956 – present

I met Fiona Fullerton, the still-stunning Bond Girl, singer and actress, at the launch of *Strictly Come Dancing* at Elstree studios in London, where she was gearing up with other celebs to learn the art of ballroom dance. To my great delight, Fiona was utterly charming and yes, beautiful in the flesh, but above all a great lady with poise and elegance.

As she came over the red carpet to be interviewed I asked if we could have a chat later and she readily agreed. It was at this sneaky private get-together where Fiona shared some of her acting stories with me.

Fiona will always be known as Bond Girl Pola Ivanova from the 1985 James Bond film *A View to a Kill*. She made her film debut in 1969 with a role in *Run Wild, Run Free*. Other big hits included *Nicholas and Alexandra* (as Anastasia), *Alice's Adventures in Wonderland* (as Alice) and *The Human Factor*, but it was on television that her star really shone. She was an original cast member on the BBC hospital drama *Angels*, which was a gritty look at life in the NHS. Fiona was stunning in a nurse's uniform and took the lion's share of all the fan mail. After that she appeared in series such as *The Charmer*, *Hold the Dream* and *To Be the Best*.

When we get to the question of the Palladium Fiona seems to light up. She starred there in 1976 as Cinderella and recalls her moment with such delight. 'It was simply unbelievable, really. I mean, the show was superb and the cast was brilliant. Every day I played the biggest and most beautiful fairytale princess of them all right there on that Palladium stage – it was enthralling.'

Referring to her cast-mates, who included Richard O'Sullivan, Richard Hearne, Yootha Joyce, Brian Murphy, Gordon and Bunny Jay and Robert Young, she said, 'Some great ponies had to pull me on three times a day in my magical carriage. The show was great fun because we had the stars of George and Mildred, plus the good-looking Richard O'Sullivan, who was a great sport and took all the lines and made people laugh.'

'There was no problem with me doing a pantomime,' she added, 'because even though I was also appearing in films and stuff like that, it was seen as a mighty feather in the cap, not least at the world famous Palladium. I am so glad I was given that opportunity.'

Anita Harris
3 June 1942 – present

Some people you meet just have star power and look like they actually enjoy the business of being on show, as it were. Anita Harris is one of them – what a star, from *Carry On* icon to pop star, great actress and great singer. She looks as good today as when she wore that famous nurse's outfit on screen, although as we take a seat to discuss her wonderful career she insists that it's not all been easy.

Anita was one of the brightest young singing stars this country had ever produced. She learned her trade from Frank Sinatra and Mae West in Las Vegas, where she was a showgirl dancer, having been talent-spotted on a London ice rink at sixteen.

Anita has worked with many golden greats including Morecambe and Wise, Harry Secombe and Tommy Cooper and has also performed alongside Dusty Springfield and Petula Clark. She graced the top of the pop charts with hits including 'Just Loving You' and became a pantomime legend as Peter Pan, but it's her appearance in uniform as seductive Nurse Clarke in 1967 film *Carry on Doctor* that is perhaps her most memorable.

She enjoyed chart hits in the 1960s and 1970s and her seasons at the London Palladium were outstanding, including seven Royal Variety Performances. Later she had a two-year run starring as Grizabella in Lloyd Webber's musical *Cats*.

'Gosh, when you say it all like that then yes, I suppose I have done a fair bit,' she laughed, 'but you know (with a twinkle in her eye), I have just loved it all. I mean, showbiz can be a good career, and look at the opportunities you are given. I count them all as blessings every day.

'I loved my time at the Palladium,' she told me with a smile. 'I know it's corny, but you really made your mark if you could say you'd appeared there. I used to get upset when the season came to a close but I always prayed that I would be back. I adore the place and it's been so good to me.

'I did a great season there with a wonderful show called *London Laughs*. It was produced by the darling Robert Nesbit, who you know had an eye for detail, but it was always glamour and simply trying to make the best show possible. I was a young girl at the time and yes, I was aware of how good the rest of the cast was, but I do think it takes time and reflection to honestly realise the privilege.

'There was super-talented Harry Secombe, who could easily have been an opera star if not for his love of comedy, and then darling Russ Conway – boy, that man could whirl up and down a keyboard with vigour – he made it all look so easy. Jimmy Tarbuck, Thora Hird, oh, so many memories – we ran for months and months back then – but the shows were really the stars because they were so well produced.'

Anita also had fond memories of another show, *To See Such Fun*, and said, 'Oh, that was another great run, with the likes of Clive Dunn – who of course played in *Dad's Army* – and then Russ Conway again, and this time we had the legend that was Tommy Cooper – he really owned the stage at the Palladium. He knew what the fans wanted and gave it to them it in spades. There really was no one like Tommy Cooper; he could turn his hand to anything. Sometimes he would just stand there on that huge Palladium stage and do nothing but shrug his shoulders as the whole place erupted. Simply brilliant to have such power. I have such fond memories thinking about us together on stage at the Palladium.'

Anita is always a lady, always a star and always bubbly, but she welled up a little when she recalled the tribute to her great pal Danny La Rue at the London Palladium. 'Well, he was a one-off for sure. What a talent. You get to thinking and looking around at the theatre and remembering all the laughs and fun you had together – I am sure many of my chums have created their own Palladium up there, aren't you?'

Adam Garcia
1 June 1973 – Present

Adam Garcia is an Australian actor and tap dancer of partial Colombian descent. He left university early to take the role of Slide in the production of the musical *Hot Shoe Shuffle*, which toured Australia for two years before transferring to London. Garcia stayed on in London to act in West End musicals.

Garcia went on to play Doody in the West End's production of *Grease* and then the illustrious Travolta character, Tony Manero, in the London stage version of *Saturday Night Fever*. Garcia reached number fifteen in the UK singles chart in 1998 with his cover version of the Bee Gees song 'Night Fever', taken from *Saturday Night Fever*. It was this smash hit musical that gave Garcia his first 'in' at the Palladium.

Adam revealed, 'I loved the film and I knew I may be in with a chance of landing the part because of my dance background. I had no idea where the show would be staged, then out of the blue they told me, "Oh, by the way, we are opening at the Palladium," and my mouth went dry. I mean, the auditions are like you see on the movies, you know. I was like, oh really? That's good, but I am sure they knew deep down that I was in shock,' he laughed.

I really liked Adam because he was so down to earth and good fun. Like so many Australians he made it all so easy. *Saturday Night Fever* did turn Adam into a star, both in London and around the world. I attended the press night and recall many people swooning and thinking he was actually better than the original, but what does Adam remember?

'Lots of hard work and stamina, because I was on stage most of that show, but I am pleased to say I totally enjoyed it and we stayed at the Palladium for over two years, so we did something right. I think now, being older and wiser,' he added, 'I get to see just what an occasion it was to appear there. I mean, looking back, you take things in your stride and forget to soak up the greater moments. I was aware of just how exciting it all was, for sure, and seeing my big image in those famous theatre boxes was more than cool, but yeah – now sometimes just walking past the theatre is a great feeling and when I look down at the stage door entrance I can easily remember getting mobbed. That was a good feeling.'

Kenneth Earle

Meeting Kenneth Earle is like meeting a legend (yes, another one). He has done the lot under the variety banner and I was fortunate to meet him at the Hippodrome in London for a chat. The Hippodrome is familiar ground for Kenneth, having appeared many times with his former and late comedy partner, Malcolm Vaughan.

Kenneth looked as sprightly as ever and I told him I often saw old variety posters with the duo's names on them. He smiled broadly and said, 'It was great, I mean, it was hard work, too, don't get me wrong, but boy, it was great fun and of course we were getting paid to do something that we both loved to do.'

Kenneth Earle and Malcom Vaughan made their first appearance at the London Palladium in *The British Record Show* in 1956. Kenneth recalled, 'We were doing well at that time and the show was a bit like a pop concert. Not because we were hip or anything, in those days you mixed the two up – but we were there at the Palladium when the big names were coming over as well, your Bob Hopes and Bings – great names.'

In fact they were pretty 'hip', with the unique sound of Vaughan's tenor voice and their well-matched humour. They enjoyed the pop explosion of their time, touring with the famous Bill Haley and the Comets in 1957 and alongside the Vic Lewis Orchestra and Desmond Lane. These were big shoes, produced by none other than Lew and Leslie Grade who were always at the sharp end of the most exciting deals. Kenneth said, 'You see, you don't know what you're part of when you're young, do you? Bill was great and the girls went wild when he came on. The theatres had seen nothing like it, really. It was all so new.'

Swept along but never taking it for granted, Earle and Vaughan were well respected among producers, including the all-important Grades and Val Parnell. They were picked by Val Parnell to take part in Independent Television's first major success, *Sunday Night at the London Palladium*, and Kenneth was clearly delighted for the opportunity to return to the great theatre.

He said with a chuckle, 'People actually rushed home from church to see the show – it was a talked-about event. That was when TV had real power and we were so thrilled to be part of it. We had the wonderful Eartha Kitt, billed as the most exciting woman on earth, and Channing Pollock, billed as the world's most beautiful man. Quite where it left us, I have no idea, but we really do have Val Parnell and Lew Grade to thank for shows like that. They broke the mould and of course made the Palladium what it is today – in my opinion, the world's greatest theatre.'

Did they have any regrets? Just one, according to Kenneth. 'Only that we both fancied the idea of becoming film stars. In a comedy vein, of course, and it would have worked, but it was the downturn of British cinema then and the birth of the beat films with Cliff and the Beatles. Don't get me wrong, I was a fan, but the type of stuff we were doing was more like Morecambe and Wise. So yeah, that would be a regret, or rather a missed opportunity, really.'

Earle and Vaughan dissolved their partnership in 1972. Vaughan's last professional work was in a summer show in Morecambe ten years later. He died in February 2014. Kenneth Earle joined the London Management agency for ten years and then set up an independent management and production agency, which continues to trade under his own name.

Petula Clark
15 November 1932 – present

Petula Clarke was born to English father Leslie Norman Clarke and Welsh mother Doris Phillips in the winter of 1932. Both parents were nurses in Surrey. As a child, Petula sang in the chapel choir and showed a skill for mimicry, impersonating Vera Lynn and Sophie Tucker for her family and friends. In 1944, Petula made her first movie and has since appeared in over thirty British and American films.

Meeting Petula is always a joy, but my first encounter was really something to remember. Petula had agreed to come along to the Westminster Millbank studios to discuss her new album and I was excited; I mean, this was Petula Clark. Even the name exudes charm, beauty, talent and fame and that's before the wonderful world-renowned hits, including 'Downtown' and 'Sleep in the Subway'.

The Millbank studios were part of Sky News and I ventured into the newsroom to enquire if anyone had seen her, as she was a tad late. To my horror and surprise she emerged from the tiny kitchen carrying a tray of teas and coffees and began dishing them up – no fuss, no diva. She said with a laugh, 'Oh, I asked for a tea and then as I was having one I decided that I would make a round and so it took off.' The girls and boys in the studio – perhaps engrossed in their own world of news flow – had no idea that this well-dressed tea lady was the super star Petula, a tale we recall and laugh about every time we meet.

Petula told me that one of her happiest memories of appearing at the London Palladium was in December 1964. It was that great title again, *Sunday Night at the London Palladium*, and she recalled with honest candour, 'Oh, it was so exciting, because my pop career had taken off again and many nice things were happening. We did the show for Mr Parnell, who was always an absolute doll, and then they presented me with my silver disc for 'Downtown'. I was breathless because as we know, in this business it's all ups and downs, and yet it's one of those moments that I really remember. At one point I was backstage in my dressing room with my father and he stood there beaming, so yeah, of course the place has special memories for me, without a doubt.'

Petula also recalled how she was envious of the very glamorous Tiller Girls and she confessed, 'It's odd, really, because when you're young you're in awe of others and they are of you, but they were all so glamorous and beautifully tall and leggy so I admired them and the dedication to their craft. They worked really hard and I never tired of seeing their famous high-kicking routine and the glittery costumes they wore. I would often have a chat with the girls, who also seemed to be in an exclusive club, you know – like a great big friendly girl gang and I loved that about them.'

Another occasion that left Petula breathless was the Royal Show in 1968, which was full of great acts and really was fit for royalty. She remembers, 'We had Eric and Ernie, plus Lionel Blair and Engelbert, but I loved the sound of Motown – I think we all did back then – so when Diana Ross and the Supremes appeared we were all over the moon. I loved the fact they loved it all so much and were really in awe of our traditions, plus the audience went crazy for them and they looked so stunning in their gowns, too. You see, that is the beauty of a royal show; you get such a mix of artistes and they all pull together to give the best performances for our royal family – it's such an honour.'

What shocked me, though, was to learn that Pet was not a fan of her early film career as a Rank Film starlet. 'I hated the hair, clothes and mostly the scripts,' she laughed heartily. There was one film in particular that she loathed – the epic movie titled *The Gay Dog*. We both laughed at how you wouldn't get away with that title now, but back then it was all about a greyhound and starred another film favourite, Wilfred Pickles. Pet said, 'I think now, looking back, it was at that time when all the other film stars appeared glamorous and well-heeled and you know, there was me in a comedy about a blooming Greyhound! But I haven't seen it for years, so maybe I am being unjust to it and it's become a classic.'

Petula as ever was kind, generous and above all a lady, and when I asked her how she would like to look back on her career she was, as ever, kind to others. 'I have worked with some great people and had some terrific songs to sing in some of the world's best venues. What more can you ask for?'

Wayne Sleep OBE
17 July 1948 – present

Wayne has appeared on television as a dancer, guest and celebrity, on shows including *I'm a Celebrity Get Me Out Of Here*, *Celebrity Come Dine with Me*, *This is Your Life*, *The Goodies*, *Parkinson*, *Wogan* and four Royal Variety Performances. He was a judge on ITV's dance show, *Stepping Out*, in 2013 and most recently was a semi-finalist in *Celebrity Master Chef*.

He is a dynamo of talent and meeting him leaves you exhausted from his own natural energy and wit, but one thing you remember; Wayne Sleep has star power and he lets you know it through one thing only, his talent.

I met Wayne at the crack of dawn while we were filming some dire pilot TV show in the old GMTV studios. The pilot was hosted by a sort-of-celebrity from the TV reality show *Big Brother*. Naturally, because Wayne was full of life at such an early hour we began to talk about our love of showbiz and in particular who and what we had worked for.

I was delighted when Wayne said, 'I have had a great time at the London Palladium and I suppose, for me, the ultimate was when we did our *Hot Shoe Show* in the theatre. It was magical and we had such a great response, so although I have enjoyed many seasons and shows there, to me, my Palladium memory would always be that one because it was my show, my name and everything just came together. It was a most beautiful time.'

Charlie Drake
19 June 1925 – 23 December 2006

Actor and comedian Charlie Drake is best remembered for his energetic slapstick comedy and pitchy catchphrase, 'Hallo, my darlings!'

I first met Charlie later in his career when he teamed up with another comedy great, Jim Davidson. The two were appearing in a rather rude version of the classic pantomime *Cinderella*. Charlie was getting on by then, but still full of fire and the confidence that had carried him through so many experiences. I was surprised when he acknowledged that any failures in his career could have been down to his 'ego', which he referred to often.

Like many of our variety heroes, Charlie came from humble beginnings. He was the uneducated son of a south London newspaper seller, but with strength of character, talent and a bucket load of confidence (that 'ego') he found fame and fortune.

His first stage appearance was at the age of eight, singing 'Any Old Iron'. After school years he did various unskilled jobs and in the evenings went round working men's clubs with a cockney patter act. He served in the RAF during the Second World War and then turned professional, becoming a noted knockabout comedian both on stage and TV throughout the 1950s.

Success fuelled his confidence and he loved the high life, with all its riches, but that ego could get the better of him and the money often ran out. He was smart, though, and when times got tough, which they did on several occasions, he managed to reinvent himself time and time again.

Despite this volatility, he earned widespread respect in the industry and that all-important place in the history books of the London Palladium, where he appeared many times, both in pantomime and as a top billing for the variety shows.

He, or maybe the 'ego', told me, 'I not only insisted on the star dressing room but demanded that it be redecorated and furnished to my own taste.' He then admitted, 'I think I enjoyed stardom but I found out quickly that it can be taken away just as fast, so why not enjoy it?'

This attitude attracted a number of powerful theatrical enemies and critics. He was keen to set the record straight, at least to some degree, or to show a humble side. 'I do think it's harder for comedians because in many respects you know that once the laughs stop it's entirely your fault, I mean, with a singer it can be said they chose the wrong song, but no, I think the comic life is far harder.'

Referring to the Palladium, he said, 'I just loved the place and felt the same about it every time. Back then, they had a great team and knew how to look after people. If you were a star they treated you like one. I knew also that the Palladium was a star on its own, really.'

That said, the Palladium was not always so good to Charlie. It was the venue for one of his less illustrious roles in an ill-advised (or maybe poorly timed) show called *Man in the Moon*.

'It was 1963,' Charlie said, 'and I was looking for something new and different to work on – a challenge, I suppose. It was a space age musical and something quite different for the festive season, and it was produced by Robert Nesbit, who was a stickler for getting it right.'

Sadly, it went very wrong and even cast members were left red-faced. The wonderful presenter Peter Purves, of *Blue Peter* and *Doctor Who* fame, told me, 'It was a disaster from day one. I was just in the chorus but it was a nightmare for nine months until we came off. Not the happiest of experiences, I do remember.'

Charlie was reflective, rather than defensive, and said, 'While I think the show had its bad points it also had its good points and truly, when you think this was 1963, well, we were just about six years too early; in 1969 we did put a man on the moon, so by rights it should have had a bleeding revival,' he laughed.

Charlie admitted that his career was hit by the failed show and there was no demand for him in film, but with that resilient ego he reminded me of his success. 'I think any artiste who has been privileged enough to play the London Palladium can rightly call themselves a star. I mean, you don't have to think you're going to return, even to play it once, but you know, I always remember going past the front of the theatre and looking up at the productions I starred in and seeing my name big in lights. I thought, whatever happens, they can't take this away from me. I would like to think I did okay at the Palladium.'

I last saw Charlie Drake where he ended his days, at Brinsworth House, a retirement home in Middlesex for actors and performers run by the Entertainment Artistes' Benevolent Fund. He did not seem bothered at all about his reduced circumstances and I would say he was a kind man who could still make you laugh out loud. He passed away on 23 December 2006.

Lulu, OBE
3 November 1948 – present

Lulu, the bonny Glaswegian Scot with the wonderful voice, has enjoyed over five decades in the limelight. Internationally renowned as a singer, actress and TV personality, she is considered a national treasure and always will be.

Lulu was born Marie McDonald McLaughlin Lawrie, the daughter of a local butcher and the eldest of four children. It seems she was 'gifted' with the ability to belt out a song from the word go, always in trouble for singing during school lessons and never short of ambition to pursue a musical career.

Lulu made her first public appearance at a coronation party at the tender age of four and said, 'From then on, I used to go in for talent competitions on my own.'

At the age of fourteen, Lulu became the lead singer of a local group, the Gleneagles, and toured local clubs in and around Glasgow and Edinburgh, including Sunday evenings at the Lindella Club where she earned £1 a night. It was here at the Lindella, on a cold Glaswegian evening, that Lulu was spotted by Marion Massey, who later became her trusted manager and mentor, guiding her to stardom.

Lulu (still Marie Lawrie) told me, 'When I was fourteen, I was very lucky. I was discovered – to use a terrible term – by a person who was absolutely sincere. Since I was five people had been coming up to me, saying, "Stick with me, baby, and I'll make you a star." In fact, nobody ever did anything for me until Marion came along.'

Marion signed Marie Lawrie and her group to a management contract and took them to London to record. She changed the group's name overnight to Lulu & the Luvvers.

Lulu flourished, with smash hit after smash hit, but in was in 1967 that she came to the famous London Palladium to appear in the Royal Variety show, with stars such as Tom Jones, Sandie Shaw and Bob Hope.

Lulu recalled, 'For a wee lassie like me, you know, to be there on a royal show at the Palladium, I was frightened to death. I think I lost a stone in weight, basically because I was shaking, but I was all right once on stage.'

Meeting Lulu is a great experience. She bounds in with the energy of someone far younger than her years and looks wonderful in person. I asked her how she manages to stay this way and she laughed and told me it's all down to her own skincare regime that she developed. 'I swear by it and I am living proof it works,' she reveals.

While we will always think of Lulu for her huge singing voice and pop stardom, we must not forget that she is far, far more. She is a movie actress, songwriter and musical icon with longevity like few others. It struck me that she is, in fact, our own Madonna, with the ability to reinvent herself at just the right time and never afraid to cross the boundaries of showbiz.

Vince Hill
16 April 1937 – present

Coventry-born singer Vince Hill is one of the best-known British singing stars and record producers of his era. A huge talent and dashingly handsome, Vince had great success as a solo recording artiste from the 1960s to the 1980s with hits including 'Take Me To Your Heart Again' (an Edith Piaf cover), 'La Vie En Rose', 'Roses of Picardy' and 'Look Around (And You'll Find Me There)'.

Yet nothing could top his mega hit cover of 'Edelweiss' from the soundtrack to *The Sound of Music*, which went to number two in the UK Singles Chart in March 1967. It confounded critics, as this was the era of flower power and a top ten dominated by the likes of the Beatles, Petula Clark, Engelbert Humperdinck and Hollies.

I met Vince thanks to another super-talent Anita Harris (bless you, Anita), and he was simply charming when he told me of his love for the Palladium. 'There was a time when I almost lived between there (the Palladium) and the Hippodrome doing late night shows. It was a wonderful period because showbiz was so much more glamorous then; people had talent and that was truly respected.'

Vince told me that his biggest Palladium thrill was to be on the same billing as the great comic Jack Benny. 'He did lots and yet nothing at all, really, but with a sigh and the lift of an eyebrow he really could make you double up with laughter. I always loved the fact I appeared with him.'

Vince also recalled the live shows at the theatre, telling me, 'It was terrifying, in a way, but when you're young you really have no idea, do you? I mean, we just got on with it and I suppose blind faith and belief carried us through.'

Vince Hill is one of life's super guys, with a wonderful voice. Most recently he has endured immense tragedy with the loss of his son. The world of variety will be thinking of him.

Russ Conway
2 September 1925 – 16 November 2000

Russ Conway was born Trevor Herbert Stanford in Bristol, England. He was the pianist who brought joy and so much happiness to so many people with his tinkling fingers and his twinkling smile. Even the PR spin said, 'Russ sent a million housewives happy and contented back to their daily chores each time they heard him on the radio.' His attractive combination of good looks and talent brought Russ Conway huge success in live concert and on vinyl and made him one of Britain's biggest-selling artistes of the 1950s and 1960s.

Looking back, it's funny how you meet these top-of-their-game guys. I bumped into Russ while attending a showbiz garden party in West London. I had been speaking to the comical duo the Cox Twins, who performed their act right there and then in front of me. They knew that someone my age had no idea who they were, but they were great fun and pretty good. At the end of the act, I showed my appreciation and turned around to find myself face to face with the man of the ivories himself, Russ Conway.

Conway spent 168 weeks in the music charts, from his first hit in 1957 with a medley called 'Party Pops' through to his 1962 winner, 'Always You and Me'. His 1959 number one record 'Side Saddle' spent an incredible thirty weeks in the charts, something he was stunned about. 'I liked the song and knew it was a hit,' Russ said, 'but I had no idea just how much of a hit it would become and boy, was I glad I found that song while working as a plugger.'

In 1957, music publisher Chappell was to bring Conway his biggest break. His boss Teddy Holmes had a new tune and no pianist, and his young employee soon came to his attention. Russ told me, 'It really was a case of just being in the right place at the right time and, you know, that is the basis of showbiz, really – luck.'

From then on it was top of the charts time and time again. Three sheet music compositions stayed at number one for a total of more than six months. He was also a hit with his TV show *At Your Request*, which ran during the late 1950s and was followed by a summer season at the Pier Pavilion in St Anne's near Blackpool. Russ said it was the mix of TV and packed houses that helped his music shoot up the charts. With a flash of that famous smile, he added, 'But that pier show was called *Let's Go Gay* – can you imagine that now?'

Russ was a true star and loved every minute of it, but he could be equally star-struck himself. He knew he was in a privileged position. 'I loved being in showbiz so much, you know. It was wonderful, because I came into it after various other jobs and so I was still in awe of it all, I mean, appearing on great stages with even greater stars; well, it was amazing for me, and while I was not a kid any more I never thought just playing the piano would lead to such great things and great people.'

His popularity endured through the seventies and eighties, perhaps not at the same level, but particularly on cruise liners and the odd TV show. He appreciates his longevity and said, 'I can't complain. I have had a great life.'

Did that 'great life' include the Palladium? Of course it did. Russ has appeared at the theatre many times and he told me of his surprise at being on a show that also starred the 'hip' pop star of the day, Sir Cliff Richard. The show was called *Stars in Their Eyes* and played in the 1960s.

'I think people were waiting for us to fall out, because all these rockers had changed the face of music in a few short years and yes, it was something of a shock, but I know that myself and Joan Regan, who was also on the bill, relished him and the Shadows being on the show as it meant one thing – a full house,' laughed Russ.

'It was great fun and we became good friends and remained so, but you see, the media even back then thought they could stir up something from nothing. In fact, we all used to go to Cliff's dressing room between shows for tea and sandwiches as he was very sociable and always had some wonderful catering in. I do recall he never actually ate that much himself, hence he kept looking great, even today.'

Russ, I remember, also told me this about the Palladium. 'As an artiste, if you are chosen to appear there then it means one thing. Basically, you have made it; that is what that theatre can do for a career.'

Adam Faith
23 June 1940 – 8 March 2003

Adam Faith was a pop star, respected businessman and money mogul. We met when I was working for a record label behind a charity song. Adam was a patron of the charity and was doing his bit to support. The record was dire and he knew it, but, ever the professional, he chose his words and facial expressions with great care to avoid any upset. Furthermore, the launch was staged at the famous Hard Rock Café – not exactly the venue he had hoped for – but with these silent and disapproving thoughts bonding us together we both got on famously.

Adam was a gentle man and, amid the confusion that goes with launching a charity single, he managed to find time to tell me about his break into the big time and that now-famous skit on the Palladium stage with TV legend Bruce Forsyth.

Adam was born Terry Nelhams on a council estate in Acton, west London. Faith was the third of five children. He left school aged fifteen to work as a messenger at Rank

Screen Services. It was in 1956 that he and some friends formed a skiffle group called the Worried Men. The band was playing in Soho, in London's West End, when Adam in particular caught the eye and ear of television producer Jack Good. Jack carried weight in the industry, having directed the BBC pop show *Six-Five Special*. As Adam told me, 'My world changed overnight, really. That was the moment it all started to take off.'

He adopted his stage name, Adam Faith, and went on to have a series of chart hits, including number one singles 'What Do You Want' and 'Poor Me'.

His success led him to the Palladium and I was chomping at the bit to hear about Bruce. 'It was the height of my pop fame, as they call it, and when it was first pitched as an idea my manager Eve was not too happy. You see, you did not cross rock and roll stars with light entertainers and that was seen as the kiss of death for your career as a pop star – for me, though, I loved it [the Palladium] and Bruce.

'We went ahead and when Bruce did a "take off" of my voice on the stage we got a lot of funny looks from the wings of the theatre. You see, I had done a deal with Bruce to pretend I was angry at this mickey-taking of my singing, and the audience was not expecting it. Even today it gets talked about.'

Adam told me, 'It was my first time at the Palladium and I was so nervous, but there was a comedian on called Beryl Reid who was fantastic and so helpful. Looking back, I was in great hands but when you're a kid you're scared. I mean, this show was the biggest thing on TV so I am glad it all went off that way, but you know who backed me? John Barry and his band the John Barry Seven, who of course is now Mr Bond,' Adam laughed.

I never saw or met Adam again, and sadly the charity single failed to bother the charts, just as he had predicted, but I will never forget our discussion and his parting advice. 'Actually, my office is in the Savoy hotel. Well, it's not my office, but I meet people there all the time and it makes them feel impressed and special. You should try it, Neil.' I did, Adam, and you're right, it does.

Johnnie Hamp
1931 – present

TV producer John Hamp, or 'Johnnie' as he is known to the showbiz world, has done so much to discover and bring new, exciting talent to the stage and screen, and I was eager to learn how he spotted future stars. Yet when we meet in the Hilton Hotel in Blackpool to discuss his wonderful career he is more taken with the view of the North Pier theatre from the hotel suite than the thought of his achievements or experiences at the Palladium. I quickly realised he was reminiscing.

'We did a record breaking run there with *The Comedians*. It was a fantastic summer, hearing two thousand people packed to the rafters roaring with laughter at the delights of Bernard, Colin and Charlie Williams. Super, great days,' he smiled.

Now retired, Johnnie is best known as one of Britain's top television producers. He is the essence of variety with experience across the sector, from his first stage appearance as a boy stooge to his magician father to his many stints as a variety artiste. Then he moved up the ranks of Granada TV to Head of Light Entertainment until he left to become his 'own man' as a movie publicist, TV presenter, theatre manager, talent booker, theatrical producer, record producer, lecturer and after dinner speaker. Nonetheless, the 'TV producer' seems to be a title he holds on to most strongly, and rightly so.

Johnnie has devised and produced more than 2,000 programmes for television and has maintained a friendly working relationship with many stars he has worked with over the years. To my sheer delight, he admitted his love affair really started with the Palladium after he got to see his favourite ever star there, Hollywood icon Danny Kaye.

John remembers, 'You see, everyone was talking about him [Danny Kaye] so I thought I would try my luck doing impressions of him myself, on stage. I recreated his act, miming to his records and routines and it seemed to work. I won the Bryan talent contest, which was a big event at that time.

'I thought he was amazing, really,' he added. 'I mean, to be able to hold an audience like that in a theatre that size – to me, as a young budding act, that was what we all aspired to do. When I went back to the Palladium to tape the *The Comedians* TV show I truly could not believe it, to be honest, not just because of the show itself but because we had managed to bring our small TV show to the West End and to the best theatre in the world, the London Palladium.'

Johnnie admitted, though, that creating the famous show was not without problems. 'It was not as simple as people think, because when you have a good comic they don't want TV, as such, because they believe it eats up material; of course, unlike today, they had to create it all. There were no scriptwriters, so the comics themselves knew they had to be on the ball and create something funny and special each week.'

Johnnie explained that when they filmed the pilot for *The Comedians* it was vastly different to anything on air at the time. Top bosses at Granada TV were less than impressed with the idea, thinking that while the show may take off in the North they had no chance with it in the rest of the country, but Johnnie had a gut feeling that it would all work out right in the end.

He managed to get *The Comedians* on air as a one-off for Granada. It was filmed before a live audience in Manchester and the audiences were directly out of the clubs, the sort of people that would sup a pint and down a pie while watching the acts.

Each comic performed for about twenty minutes and then they were edited together into half-hour shows. Each edition featured up to ten stand-up comics and as Bernard Manning, the star of the show, recalled rather cruelly, 'Fine for me as I had lots of material but others, well, after one week they were shot as they had nothing to come back for.'

It was an immediate success and was fully commissioned for a series. The popularity continued, with many jokes finding their way into local acts or the pockets of pub goers, who finally had a TV show that the ordinary working man could really relate to. An LP record of the show reached the best-seller charts and became such a success that it is now extremely rare and valuable. The record label planned to market all the acts and do various albums of the stars, but it was, as ever, Bernard Manning who took off with the very first bestselling comedy LPs.

The format of *The Comedians* was rarely changed – just the addition of the Pamela Davis dancers for live performances. The show enjoyed success at the Palladium, a Royal Gala performance, several sell-out national tours and the Critics' Circle Award, all of which left its creator stunned.

Reflecting, Johnnie said, 'I think, looking back, I had no idea just how big it would be. When we got to the Palladium everyone who had booked us was worried, you see, because with comics like Charlie Williams, who was very Barnsley in his accent and straight, direct northern, well, they worried that no one would actually understand him and the others. I know talking to them they were all a bit concerned too.'

So why did it work? Johnnie continued, 'I think it's down to human nature, really. I mean, the lads were funny – I knew that. When you look at it I think, well, people said Max Miller only did well down South but it was not the case, as he appeared at Leeds and Nottingham Empires to great success and, of course, he was very London in his humour.'

Charlie Williams confirmed the early concern among many of the acts, telling me, 'Nay, lad, we were all worried, you see, because only a few months earlier, like, I was just doing clubs for five pounds and such, so yeah, this was a big deal. But Johnnie our producer always believed in us, like, he told us we could do it and so I suppose we all thought we could.'

Johnnie told me that while the first run at the Palladium was originally only a short one, the show and its word of mouth became so successful that it was finally extended until it reached six months. 'I know, crazy, looking back, but they were all calling the boys the new 'Crazy Gang' and you know, the good thing is that they all got on and were all really just wanting to create and give a fantastic show. It appears that even the royal family were *Comedians* fans, which was great.'

The show by this time was a massive success, without much PR, either. It was a wonderful position for a producer to be in, with a group of guys telling jokes and filling the venue every night.

In the mid-eighties, Johnnie Hamp left Granada and set up his own independent production company, John Hamp Enterprises, to produce programmes for Granada and the cable-satellite Super Channel. He used this post-Granada 'retirement' to take up his love of oil painting, and his works are now in great demand – a talented man indeed.

Johnnie was a wonderful guest. As he got up to leave the suite he said to me, 'Look, the Pier theatre is now all lit up! Oh, how nice. I used to love going down to the theatre when the lights were on, you know, it made it feel all the more special. I know the boys loved the Palladium but they also loved that Pier theatre, too – it was the start of everything for us there.'

Danny Kaye
18 January 1913 – 3 March 1987

Danny Kaye was born in Brooklyn, New York. He made his Broadway debut in *The Straw Hat Review* in 1939. In the forties and fifties, he appeared in musicals and other films. During the sixties, he had his own TV show and throughout the seventies he focussed mainly on charity work. He took a few TV roles in the 1980s before suffering a fatal heart attack in Los Angeles in March 1987.

Danny was as big as any pop star today and filled the Palladium for weeks and weeks through his talent of comedy, singing and dancing; there was also the memorable showbiz moment where he requested and received a cup of tea on stage, much to the delight of the audience.

Bryan Michie

The well-known show business impresario Bryan Michie made regular tours across Britain seeking young talent. It was while searching for young talent in the north of England in 1938 that Bryan discovered Ernie Wise of Morecambe and Wise fame. He mounted talent shows in theatres and cinemas across the country during the 1940s and 1950s, which continued throughout his career. In 1962, Bryan produced a television talent show called *Now's Your Chance*.

Ernie Wise
27 November 1925 – 21 March 1999

Ernie Wise is, in my mind, vastly underrated as an entertainer and while he is held in great esteem by the public he is often referred to as the straight man to the comedy genius of Eric Morecambe. I myself was lucky enough to meet Ernie during his return to the West End in a musical comedy at the Savoy theatre called *The Mystery of Edwin Drood*. He was, as I recall, dapper, warm and very funny, but he did look at odds with what was going on around him and seemed to be a bit lost. The show also starred Lulu and was being billed as the biggest event of that season, but after speaking with Ernie he told me that he had some reservations about certain aspects of the show. These were to be proved correct, as it just lasted ten weeks.

As we settled down to start the interview he knew what the question was going to be – and about whom – so I steered away from Eric and asked him what it was about stage performing that still gave him a thrill. His response did not shock me, but I do remember him coming alive at the prospect of getting back up on stage and as he said, 'Doing my thing.'

Eric went on to say, 'I do enjoy this type of work, because it's a discipline for me, you see. I can't adlib and I can't stray away from the script. Most actors loathe working with us variety turns as we always want to turn something into a laugh; that is a temptation, but on the other had we always want to give value for money and I always feel if people have had a laugh then that is half the battle, don't you agree?

'I always loved doing variety and every aspect of it,' he continued, 'simply because I loved the travel, the new adventures and, of course, the challenge of making people laugh. It was not always easy and I know that Eric worried terribly about it but, you see, I am a Yorkshire man and we take stuff in our stride, don't we? So no, it was never a problem for me, really.'

I asked Ernie to recall his first stint at the Palladium and it was like someone had shone a torch on his face. He looked decades younger and began to sparkle. Seriously, he loved speaking about that time, and told me, 'We were with Ernie Ford, who was a huge pop star at that time. One thing me and Eric always said was that if we made the Palladium we had in fact made it, which was true of course, but then we went and made that TV show *Running Wild* and ruined it again,' he laughed.

'It was always such a buzz, even if it was just our shows, but doing the Royals – oh, they were wonderful, because we were working with our heroes. It was really that exciting, and to be in that place! We loved all the halls, really – even Glasgow Empire, to a degree – but yes, looking back, I think we both agreed that doing our first big thing there was when it really began to take off.'

There is a statue of Ernie, now, in his home town of Morley, the town where he won his first ever talent contest. It's a beauty, but it's also sad that the whole project had to be funded by the family. After all, he gave us all so much pleasure. Why on earth could someone from the area not have thought this was a good idea?

I asked Ernie how he would like to be remembered and he said simply, 'If you can say, "He played all his favourite theatres and made people smile," then that is how I would like to be remembered. I think it's a good thing to leave behind, don't you?'

And he did make us laugh.

Jim Davidson OBE
13 December 1953 – present

A lot has been written and said about the comedian Jim Davidson over the last few years and so much of his talent has now been disregarded. He shot to fame after appearing on the TV talent show *New Faces* and became a staple of TV shows and sitcoms, as well as the host of *The Generation Game*, but Jim remembers the Palladium with affection. 'I did a great panto there in the eighties with Mollie Sugden, Windsor Davies, Lionel Blair and Melvyn Hayes called *Dick Whittington*. It was still cool then to do panto and summer seasons,' he laughed.

Jim fondest memories of the Palladium, apart from the cast and crew, were the stage staff and the people who worked at the theatre. 'They made you feel welcome and that you were the biggest star to ever have come through that door. It's amazing, really, because everyone has, yet the season was a record breaker. Yes, I think I did get a little lump in my throat every time I walked out on that stage. I defy anyone to not feel the same; it's the place where so much entertainment history has taken place and that is why it's special.'

Today, Jim is much the elder statesmen of comedy. After appearing on and winning the reality TV show *Big Brother*, he admitted that this is the 'third act – the rebirth'. He also told me, however, that his dream would still be to produce and star in his own show again in London – and yes, 'It would have to be at the Palladium. I don't think we will have to wait too much longer.'

Larry Grayson
31 August 1923 – 7 January 1995

Larry Grayson was a one-off, a true star. He brought high camp to television in the seventies with his catchphrases – 'Shut that door!' and 'What a gay day!' – and his references to fictional characters such as Everard, Slack Alice and Apricot Lil, delivered with pursed lips and hand-on-hip flouncing. The characters were, of course, all made up and people loved him for it, yet he revealed that 'people asked after them as if they were real, you know, so in the end they had me believing too'.

After spending much of his career in variety, Grayson found his greatest fame on television as host of *The Generation Game*, taking over from Bruce Forsyth and finding popularity with the game show, which featured relatives of different generations and a host of prizes.

Larry really had to wait until 1972, when he performed in front of the queen in the Royal Variety Gala at the London Palladium, in aid of the Olympics Fund, and was named the Variety Club of Great Britain's Show Business Personality of the Year. Stardom had finally come his way in middle age. He spoke then of being an overnight success.

Larry was my inspiration in comedy terms, because he seemed nice and everyone loved him. People liked him to the point you could not take offence at all. I enjoyed meeting him and as ever, he was revealing, kind, sharing and above all inspiring, because he simply said, 'If you think you're funny then don't let anyone else say you're not. Prove that you are.'

The uniqueness of Larry and what made him watchable were his charming quirks and highly quotable catchphrases. Coming out on to the stage, he would launch into an anecdote then stop momentarily to complain he was feeling 'giddy', or that there was a draft coming from the wings. This would convulse the audience into stitches and he knew it. He looks at the audience with such a knowing stare and then he added the final icing on the cake – a cry of 'Shut that door!'. Larry was not like other comics I met. He was cheerful, kind and fun and it was like having a gossip with someone you had known for years.

I first met Larry as a kid when he was starring for the summer season up in Blackpool; the thing I recall most was the fact that, unlike most stars, he did not hide away and slide into stage doors with dark glasses. He 'arrived', so that all his fans could see him, and of course those without tickets he charmed in; he did his own PR and loved it. I would say he knew the value of how to win people over. I often stood by my dad as he and Larry chatted about the other shows, the box office and who was doing what with whom.

Larry never spoke down to you as a child, though. He spoke to you in an adult way and made you feel important and part of the conversation. I remember him telling me, while we sat looking at the North Sea, 'You have to remember, people on holiday have to be given a good show as this may be the only two weeks of the year they get away. It's vital they go back having enjoyed the show. Do you understand?' Put that way, I did, and he was gentle with it too, explaining how the audience were in fact your pay packet, because, 'Without them you're really nothing. You can't be without them because you need them more than they need you.'

Hypochondria was Larry's stock in trade, too, because he actually believed he was ill all the time. I would often hear him say to Dad, 'I feel terrible, honest, I am exhausted. It's been nonstop all night.' We laughed, but he was serious – or was he testing out new material? It was used in his act to gain sympathy from the audience, thus he was constantly feeling 'as limp as a vicar's handshake' and coming over 'all queer'. This brought even more howls of laughter.

I met Larry many times and I recall him still being excited by the fact he had been starring at the London Palladium. As he put it, 'I never thought it would happen, you see, because I had got to the age when you think, oh well, that has passed over – you do, you just sigh and think, well, it would have been nice.'

Larry was in a magical mood speaking about his shows there. He revealed that his success was all the more sweeter for having his favourite actress, Noele Gordon, on the show. 'She was wonderful. You know, people think she was just this soap star but she could do the lot and really turn a heel, you know – amazing, really.'

Larry confessed that while he loved being on the famous stage the one star in particular that fascinated him was the late great Judy Garland, whose songs he used as intro music when coming on stage. 'I thought she was marvellous, you know. Such a star. I saw her in London and Birmingham when she first came over and she had it all, for me – I was transfixed, to be honest, so starring on the same stage as her, well, it was beyond dreams,' he laughed.

Larry also was old-school in many ways; he admitted to me that he would have loved a crack at the movies. 'I think to be on a movie set would have been great. I grew up on all those movies, you know – Alice Faye, Ginger Rogers – so yes, I suppose even a *Carry On* would have been good. They don't make the films I like now, but then, everything moves on.'

While Larry was at the Palladium he also had a young comic who is still going strong today, the one and only Keith Harris and Orville the duck. Keith also remembers the season. 'It was great, a smashing time. You respected the top of the bills back then because they had worked hard to get there, so it was always, "Evening, Mr Grayson," and he would be ever so sweet and say, "Call me Larry." That was respect, and I think it's a shame now that it's all gone.'

Larry told me that he never felt it was work while at the Palladium. 'We had full houses, you see, and because of the fact that audience there, the way it's built, they feel they are right with you – well, half the battle is won. It was a great time in my life and yes, I adored being at the theatre.'

Tony Hatch
30 June 1939 – present

In my showbiz career I have been fortunate to work with some of the best songwriters in the business. Some, such as Stock, Aitken and Waterman, have an 'era', when their melodies, key selections and song structures offer a formula that can be repeated time and time again until the audience tire. Others do very well but sit below the glitz of the showbiz radar and for me this includes perhaps one of our best and most underrated tunesmiths, Tony Hatch.

Tony, a pianist, arranger and producer, is a unique one-man hit machine. He penned his first hit, 'Look For A Star', at the age of twenty and went on to write dozens of themes and scores for TV shows such as *Crossroads*, *Emmerdale*, *The Sweeney*, *Mr & Mrs* and that Australian smash hit *Neighbours*. In fact, *Neighbours* is now the most played soap opera theme tune in the world after *Coronation Street*. He also wrote or produced for bands and artistes such as the Searchers, David Bowie and Petula Clark, as well as scores for film and stage music.

His back catalogue runs to more than 1,000 credits, including more than 750 songs and the production of nearly 200 singles and albums. It is no surprise that Tony was chosen as a judge on the TV show *New Faces* and, of course, only right that he found himself at the London Palladium – a privilege truly earned and deserved.

Meeting Tony was like meeting an array of your favourite artistes all at one time, because he has given us so many of the great theme tunes we know today. I was expecting the Mr Nasty character he portrayed in *New Faces* (he preceded Simon Cowell with his blunt opinions), but to my surprise he was incredibly down to earth and easy to chat to.

He laughed and said, 'I know, I think looking back I was so lucky in a way. I could be direct and slightly revealing for the simple reason I was a song writer and producer, so in the end I had no reason to be that nice, because I was not a fellow artiste.'

I asked him about today's artistes and he cites the difference, in his view. 'I worked for the late great Sir Lew Grade at ATV, who was a mega star himself and, of course, ran so many entertainment areas, but that was it. I worked for them, whereas today someone can own their own TV show and create a worldwide format as well as be the star, which was unheard of in my day. Truthfully, I am not sure I would be that inclined to take all that on, really.'

We were speaking at the launch of a London musical with a sixties theme, which naturally included lots of Tony's songs like 'Call Me' and 'Downtown'. 'Ah, yes,' he says with a smile, 'I think people associate me with the sixties but I had hits in every decade. For me, it's always been about the music.'

It was in the late sixties that Tony appeared for the first time at the Palladium, together with Jackie Trent, his then wife and co-songwriter, and Max Bygraves. 'We had some success by then,' he said, 'and you know, to be appearing in that venue, well. The show itself was built around Max and we were the guest stars, but Jackie and I really enjoyed the experience. I mean, to sing your own songs and play a piano on the stage of the Palladium. Dream come true. And yes, we were in awe, but then I have always loved the old-time variety stuff.

'The late great Arthur Worsley was also on the bill,' he added, 'and he was just as excited as the first time he had appeared, so it had that kind of appeal. I think to Max Bygraves we were just the young hip pop duo, although I felt it was something more, in the sense that the reaction from the crowd every night was amazing. We loved Max, though, and he was a real crowd puller. I do think that is what people forget, now – on that stage every night was so much talent and he had it in spades.

'I also remember the crowds outside the theatre. It was an amazing time and we were lucky enough to go back on quite a few occasions to perform, but for me, it does not matter if it's me or an artiste performing one of my songs, I still pinch myself hearing the orchestra at the Palladium striking up one of the tunes I dreamed up. It's always a huge thrill.'

Tommy Trinder
24 March 1909 – 10 July 1989

Perhaps one man who symbolised the success of the London Palladium in the 1940s and fifties was none other than the late and simply wonderful comedian Tommy Trinder.

I met Tommy towards the end of his life, in the 1980s, when he was doing a series for Channel 4 and enjoying several invitations to showbiz events and affairs of the time. He was always charming, quick witted and confident and, like the great trouper that he was, always planning the next joke and comeback – normally in that order.

Tommy did seem surprised that I would remember him – I was still at school – but I had grown up with dinner-time conversations laden with wonderful names from comedy and variety. Tommy was often in a regaling mood and equally unforgiving about fellow comics but, looking back, his views were honest and often right.

Tommy told me that when he hosted *Sunday Night at the London Palladium*, it was truly groundbreaking. 'Nothing like that had been on TV before. It was a first; we gave the public big stars and yes, it was free, so looking back it did help to kill off variety, in a way, but then it also helped it too.'

Tommy told me that the best thing about appearing at the Palladium was not just the money, although he admitted he loved that side of it, but the stunts. 'I loved doing stunts to keep my name in the press and of course, I wrote my own shows, so I had to be good. I did one where I had money printed with my face on it and it became a collector's item.'

Tommy revealed that he was cautious about his replacement, Bruce Forsyth, on the show after he had left. 'I think, looking back, you have a time. Val (Parnell) had some other ideas different to mine, plus, like everything in this job, he was cheaper and whatever showbiz is, it's cheap.'

Tommy looked like he had never aged and I do remember that people sought his opinion on everything and everyone. My abiding memory is that when I told him I wanted to continue a career in showbiz he said, in no uncertain terms, 'Go for it and don't let the buggers put you off, because if they do, you know, they have won.'

I have stuck to this advice ever since. Thanks, Tommy.

Aimi MacDonald
27 February 1942 – present

Aimi MacDonald began as a dancer with Le Charley Ballet Company playing major venues in Paris and Las Vegas. Her first big West End break and musical was *On the Town* in 1963, directed by Joe Layton; she also featured in many cabaret performances in leading West End nightspots.

Aimi was spotted by Marty Feldman and John Cleese and became a household name following her performance in the television show *At Last the 1948 Show*, which was produced by the late great Sir David Frost.

Aimi was something of a childhood icon to me, as I recall her popping up on many TV shows when there were just the three channels. She seemed glamorous and good fun with an easy smile, always ready to laugh at herself. Finally getting to interview her was a real treat.

She told me that when appearing as a Las Vegas showgirl dancer she actually met the king of rock and roll, Elvis Presley, but in her typical way downplayed this historic moment in her young life. 'Darling,' she said, 'he was wonderful. He had finished his show on the strip and gone down to this jazz club where all the acts played after their own shows and, you know, played the music they really enjoyed. So yeah, it was a funky time,' she giggled.

I asked Aimi if she found him attractive and she replied, 'Did I think he was good looking? Well yes, in a way, as he had really nice skin and was ever so polite and things like that, but I was just awestruck, darling. I mean, this was the king of rock and roll and, you know, I had his records and posters on my wall.'

'He had on a lot of mascara,' she added, 'and that stunned me, really. I did think, why is this man wearing mascara? But as someone pointed out, well, he wears it when he's performing. But it was a shock to a young girl like me.'

Aimi has happy memories of her big Royal Variety show in November 1968. 'Oh, it was magical, you see, because at that time I was starring in *The Mating Game* with the darling Lionel Blair. That's when I felt I was a star. My name was outside the theatre in lights and that was my ambition – to appear in a theatre with my name in lights – so yes, I finally felt I had made it, as they say.'

Aimi also let slip that her TV pal John Cleese came to see her in the show, before he had hit the dizzy heights of fame himself. He asked her, 'What is it like to be a star, then?' – a question she finds amusing, even today. 'When you look at what he then went on to, you have to agree it was a rather strange question to be asked,' she mused.

So did she enjoy the Royal Variety show and the Palladium?

'It was nerve wracking because we were performing in front of Her Majesty Queen Elizabeth, the Queen Mother,

Princes Charles, Princess Anne, Princess Margaret and the Earl of Snowdon and, of course, there was a big level of security all around the theatre.'

Aimi remembered bumping into comedy greats Eric and Ernie in the corridor of the Palladium. 'They were just the funniest people both on and off stage, but even then, I worried about Eric. He seemed never to switch off and worried about everything and everyone, actually. Such a nice guy.'

Aimi became something of a regular at the Royal Variety shows and in one she worked with Ethel Mermen and Howard Keel. She described Howard as 'simply the manliest man ever. I watched all his movies and was totally smitten by him, really'.

One of her greatest memories came from behind the scenes, after the show when the acts are introduced to the royals. 'I just remember Ethel and the Queen Mother gossiping for ages like Cissie and Ada, the Les Dawson character. You know, just chatting away like two women do; it made many of us laugh because it all seemed so normal. That is what you get at a Royal show, lots of nerves and backstage flutters but then, afterwards, this gem of a scene between two people who respected each other, basically.'

Bob Monkhouse
1 June 1928 – 29 December 2003

Bob Monkhouse was, without doubt, one of Britain's most prolific and best-known entertainers of his time, with a career that lasted for over fifty years. He is multitalented – a cartoonist, comedian, actor, and writer and TV presenter – and was known as the ultimate master of the slick one-liner, with a huge collection of jokes. He never stopped jotting down new gags to add to his 'book', as he called it. In the short time of our interview he added six to that book.

Bob was often criticised by some for what they saw as his super-smooth on-screen persona, complete with permanent suntan and fake smile, yet he remained popular for decades and even now, repeats of his shows still gain huge ratings. Bob was often described as a 'British Bob Hope', which he loved. He told me, 'To be honest, he was a hero of mine and it's a not a bad thing to be called is it?'

Bob was a regular on hit radio shows such as *Variety Bandbox* and *Workers Playtime* and became one of the first comedians to be given a contract with the BBC. He formed a successful partnership with Denis Goodwin and they wrote for such stars as Arthur Askey, Ted Ray, Bob Hope, Jack Benny, Dean Martin and Jerry Lewis, pouring out more than 2,000 radio scripts. Commenting on this role, Bob said, 'I treated it as a factory job, really. I was very determined and knew what I had to achieve that day and that meant that, as a factory, we had to get jokes out and they had to be good jokes. It was a very successful partnership, though – I truly loved Denis.'

Meeting Bob was truly memorable. I was working at a radio station in London at the time, where guests would arrive each day to speak on the breakfast show. Bob was there to plug his new joke book and I was lined up to chat to him after his breakfast slot, down in the TV studio.

Bob came off air and I was ready to go but he decided

he wanted to have a bit of breakfast before we started our interview, so I placed him in the staff canteen and ordered his breakfast. Just as it arrived, Bob took a call on his mobile, so I sat back and relaxed; however, as the waitress was about to place the eggs and bacon down on the table she was 'goosed' by a fellow radio presenter and the whole lot slid off the tray straight on to Bob's immaculate tailoring, a very light blue suit.

I jumped up to stop it, but in doing so I managed to knock the full cup of black coffee all over him too. It was like a moment in a movie when everything stops and we all just sat there gasping with mouths open.

We mopped up as best we could, but an egg and bacon suit with dash of coffee was unlikely to offer much comfort. To my relief, Bob, ever the professional, was still willing to do the interview wearing a radio station t-shirt. It did little to flatter his fuller figure at the time but nonetheless he was a pro, so we carried on the best we could.

Bob told me about every aspect of his showbiz life, which was truly bulging with variety. He had done it all and he loved to recall how he sold jokes to esteemed comedians who he respected and looked up to. Bob said it was extra special when they paid.

'Of course, I was cheeky,' he said. 'I mean, you had to be, but yes, I used to stand outside the stage door of the Palladium hoping to sell jokes to the likes of Tommy Trinder, Arthur Askey and the like. They all liked to give the impression that they did not need a script writer, but we all need help, so when they saw this young kid being pushy with his good jokes – well, if they were useful, why not take a few? That is how my joke-selling career really took off.'

Bob told me that his stamina as a stand-up comic was quite simple really. 'I was able to remember my own jokes – I had created them. That was the best thing. So it was easy, really.'

Bob told me of his stints at the London Palladium hosting the *Sunday Night* show. He gave praise to many others who gave him the big break on this epic TV show, including Lew Grade. 'Lew was a wonderful man, because he loved talent; that was the thing about him. If you had it or he thought you had it, then you were in. Lew told me I would be great hosting the show and, you know, he was right. It was the one big turning point in my career.'

Bob admitted, though, that many performers on the show were overcome by nerves. 'Oh, I seemed to get them all because, you know, it was live, and then they would have all kinds of tummy trouble and funny turns. My biggest fear was when looking into the wings of the London Palladium and just hoping that they were standing there and thinking, please god, be there, as it will look awful for the audience if you're not.'

Bob also let slip that the Royal Variety shows are a riot backstage, not before the show, but after. 'You see, you're in the greatest theatre in the world, at the Palladium, and nerves are aplenty. Then once the act had been on their "ego" would return and they would go around dispensing advice on the audience, clearly forgetting their own nerves only six minutes prior to this. That is my abiding memory of the Palladium, really.'

Bob was the ultimate gentleman and he told me one

last comedy gem. 'I love Joan Rivers. She, to me, has it all, you know – wonderful timing and some great comic creations, her and Phyllis Diller. They never fail to make me laugh.'

Joan Rivers
8 June 1933 – 4 September 2014

Joan Rivers got her big break in 1965, a booking on *The Tonight Show Starring Johnny Carson*. She became an instant hit and landed her first syndicated talk show on daytime television, *That Show with Joan Rivers*. This, combined with appearances on *Carson* and *The Ed Sullivan Show*, made Rivers a household name.

Meeting Joan was like having a meeting with an ideas-hurricane. She never stopped, from adlibs to new designer ranges for a shopping channel; the constant touring around the world with all her material made you feel like a slacker, but Joan was funny, gracious and rather revealing, as I have found out many times.

Joan told me that she first became aware of the London Palladium 'simply because I am that old; I mean, I was there when they laid the foundation stone', she joked. On a more serious note, she told me, 'It was when all our big US stars came over to appear there in the 1950s – that's when I truly began to aspire to the place as somewhere I would one day perform,' she confided.

The Palladium, she told me, was the ultimate theatre for her show and she loved the venue so much she recorded her bestselling DVD there. 'I am lucky, because my dreams came true. When I was recording my DVD

I remember taking it all in and looking at the vast auditorium, knowing who had stood right there and looked out onto a vast arena of people laughing, or in my case, looking puzzled,' she joked.

Joan said that in the US it is still a performer's dream to play the venue. 'Absolutely. I mean, I got so much more work just because I appeared there; people then wanted to book me onto chat shows and talk about the theatre's history and such like.'

Joan admitted that she had a few royal fans, in particular Prince Charles and the lovely Camilla, Duchess of Windsor. 'She uses all my skincare range, truly she does and it's a great range, look at her – she looks wonderful.' She added, 'Prince Charles, who is a great pal, told me that he too loved going to the Palladium and assured me that the audiences there would love me. He said, "Just look at the place and enjoy the moment." I took his advice and it all worked out fine.'

Joan told me that she would love to play the venue when she reached the ripe old age of 100 years. 'I am planning to book the venue and, for sure, I know George Burns almost made it but I plan to beat him and actually do it,' she laughed.

I spoke with Joan as I normally did, prior to her UK tour, about two weeks before her death; as ever, she was in fine form. We gossiped about her new range at QVC and her plans to return to acting. One thing I will always remember about Joan is that she really was an expert at plugging herself and all future projects. She mentioned everything ahead of the chat, so it went like this. 'I have just dashed back from *Fashion Police* – we were taping today and it went so well. We had great guests on and yes, Cher has agreed to come on – it's top secret though, you know.'

This was pure Joan, telling you a nugget and informing you she is in demand. Hopefully you would tweet, Facebook or simply gossip about it, which kept her in the news.

During our last chat, she spoke of walking out of a CNN interview simply because, 'I have a new book to plug and you know, the girl was nice but dim and I figured, look I am eighty-one – how much time do I have to waste?' She typically turned everything into a joke and a figure of fun.

Joan could be serious, though, and spoke often during our chats of her loneliness. Not showbiz-lonely, but as she said, 'It's like the Madonna song "Take a Bow". It's great when you're up there making them laugh and all that, but I come home alone to my dogs – I never saw it working out like this, you know. I am a Jew for goodness sake! I figured I may just meet someone and get married again.' Joan also spoke about the death of her husband Edgar. 'I don't have much sympathy, in that I miss him and think now of all the good times he has missed out on by being a chicken and leaving us all way too early. All the heartache is tough to deal with,' she added.

It was odd now, looking back, that Joan had less than two weeks to live herself; yet, as ever, she was bouncy fun and above all thinking of others. 'I have a few problems with my voice. It's annoying, as I have perfect health but the tool that I need the most – my voice – seems to be giving up on me and yet all I get told is to rest and ease up. Why?' she snapped. 'I mean, I have good health but maybe the voice will give me up. Then I'll be like Helen Keller, doing the act with cue cards and boys holding them up,' she laughed.

I owe such a great favour to Joan, too, as she was encouraging to me in my return to stand up and quietly came along to a stand up night while in London. I casually mentioned it to her and she just arrived very quietly at the back and, when I'd finished, told me, 'You're funny. Take it from me, you're funny,' and with that, helped me shape the next stage of my career. How many people in this job would take the time to do that?

Joan also wanted me to guest on her reality TV show, offering media training and basically camping it up. 'You'll be great!' We also made plans to appear on her own show, *In Bed with Joan*; even now, looking back at that final call, I recall asking her how she would like to be remembered and quick as a flash she asked, 'You taping this?' I was, and she quickly said, 'Well, truthfully, to be remembered at all is the one thing we can only dream of. So yeah, to be remembered as a comic – someone who made people smile and maybe, once in a while, laugh.'

When I read the news of Joan's accident and then passing – it takes a lot to make a hardened showbiz reporter like me quake, but I admit, I shed a tear for my pal Joan. No, not pal; actually she was a leader, a trail blazer, and above all else there will never be anyone quite like Joan Rivers again.

Simon Cowell
7 October 1959 – present

Now, Simon Cowell is one of today's mega moguls, as we all know, thanks largely to hit shows like *X Factor* and *Britain's Got Talent* and their string of global formats. However, my association goes way back, when we worked together on projects for Mike Stock and Matt Aitken, the famous record producers who along with Pete Waterman created hits for many of Simon's acts long before he found fame on TV.

Simon is certainly a showman and he readily admits that he loves the new side of fame that his success has produced. I myself thank him for my association with some of his hit songs for acts such as Robson & Jerome, the Gladiators and even the boxer Frank Bruno.

It came as a shock to no one when the producer Mike Stock finally revealed in the media that Robson & Jerome were not in fact the greatest singers in the world and their success was down to ghosted vocalists at the studios. I remember this session well – but perhaps it offers a story for my next book.

Simon, however, has enjoyed huge success via the Royal Variety show, thanks to his prize of performing in front of the royal family for winners of *Britain's Got Talent*. He revealed, 'You know, when I was younger I used to enjoy watching the Royal Variety show from the London Palladium and it was an event – a big event – so when I was looking at the ultimate prize for the winner it appeared to be the best one in my book. What greater honour, really, than to perform on the stage at the London Palladium in front of the royals?'

I still work with Simon quite regularly as he has used my studios at various points during the *Britain's Got Talent* series, including coverage for the runners-up. Susan Boyle came directly to the studios after her final show, to beam round the world via camera. Now Susan, whom I have since interviewed, told me her one dream about being on the show. 'I did not win, I know that, but I told Simon if he can get me on the Royal show and at the Palladium then truly all my dreams will have come true.'

It seems Simon was right to choose the Palladium and the Royal Variety show as his number one prize. 'Just going into the Palladium gives you goose bumps,' he said. 'There truly isn't a theatre in the world like it.'

His passion for the theatre was clear when he managed to book it for a new project, his first musical with the title *I Can't Sing*. He may readily admit that this project was not one of his best. The show closed due to poor ticket sales and unfavourable reviews, but Simon is used to taking a punt. It wasn't his first and won't be his last.

Tom Fletcher
17 July 1985 – present

McFly singer and songwriter Tom Fletcher started out as a budding musical theatre talent and hopeful, training at the famous Sylvia Young Theatre School in London. At the age of ten he landed the role of Oliver in the eponymous musical at the London Palladium. He told me of his memories of appearing on such a hit show.

'It was a natural and thrilling progression for me, actually, because I was going to a theatre school. I looked at it as great opportunity to learn some stage-craft. I know that sounds big-headed now but I do think that when you go to these types of schools you grow up pretty fast. I mean, loads of people went to my school and found great success after leaving. That is hopefully what you train for.'

Tom has fond memories of working with the star of the show, Jim Dale, who was playing Fagin in the musical. 'I knew he was a massive star, but he was also nothing but kind and really helpful. I was only ten in the show at that time; I guess I got it because I looked angelic. That is a word I kept hearing but I loved it. I mean, to be on stage every night in that theatre, the London Palladium, well – thanks to that I knew what I wanted to do as a career. I often look back at that period as a turning point even though I was young. I think the combination of such a great musical and a star like Jim made you think, yeah anything is possible, really.'

Tom, who is now also a children's author and composer of hits for many other boy bands, including One Direction, told me, 'To appear at the Palladium is a feather in any performer's cap, but I was so lucky. I mean, just ten years old and on that stage. Even now I shudder to think where that confidence came from.'

Linford Hudson – Mr Palladium

There is an old saying in the world of theatre – 'Look after the sound and lights and they will look after you.' No one knows this better than the 'follow spot' man himself, Linford Hudson.

For those new to theatre talk, a 'follow spot' is a luminaire operated by a skilled technician to light a specific performer as they move about the stage.

Linford is rightly known as the 'King of the Follow Spot' at the Palladium and has been there for over fifty years. It was such an honour to meet and interview him, as he has literally seen it all. We sat down in the Val Parnell bar to start our interview and, I must admit, it was truly a dream come true.

It turns out that Linford is rather shy of me and appears a tad nervous of the lights and cameras set up around us for the interview. I realised he is used to beaming the light down on others, rather than being in the centre of it. To defuse his worries I loosely talk about his career and, unknown to him, start recording, so that it gives the feeling of a friendly chat rather than an interview.

Linford's first big Palladium show was in May 1963. The production was called *Swing Along*, starring Tony Hancock. Linford told me, 'He was a funny man and people really enjoyed the show. I have no doubt he was a comic genius but he was very sad along the way, which was heart-breaking at time.'

Linford's list of follow spot stars reads like a showbiz directory, with the likes of Sammy Davis Junior, Frank Sinatra, Liza Minnelli, Tommy Cooper, Sarah Vaughan, Josephine Baker, Bette Davis, Ella Fitzgerald ... I could go on and on and on. It is a treasured roll call of true talent and celebrity and, moreover, he has stories about most of them.

Judy Garland's show in 1964 was another of Linford's first follow spot jobs. 'She was a true artiste, in my opinion,' he told me. 'I never met her in person, which was a shame, as I truly loved bringing the spotlight down on her and she knew how to react to it. But when they are great, they are great – and she, to me, was a Palladium great. I have met her daughters and done the same for them and they are lovely, such nice ladies; you can see the talent the mother passed on to them, without question.'

Linford is a naturally shy man but you can imagine he has few inhibitions in his domain of the spotlight box, his most natural, familiar and comfortable working habitat. When we film him changing a light bulb in the foyer this comes to the fore, as he offers to change it three times so that we get the 'best shots'. It was a lovely moment to work with someone who understands completely what you need.

To my good fortune, Linford's nerves settled and he was in a great revealing mood. He continued, 'I've also lit Lena Horne, Julie Andrews, Ginger Rogers, Carmen Miranda, Carrie Fisher and Frank (Sinatra). Frank was wonderful and so appreciative of your work for him. He knew that the light man could make you look great and, you know, he was a huge tipper too – that made my day, really,' he laughed.

One of Linford's heroes was the late, great and super talented Sammy David Jr, who starred at the theatre in a musical called *Golden Boy* (1968). 'What a wonderful time I had,' said Linford. 'I met all his bodyguards and yet I never saw any trouble with him at all. I think it was a thing he was used to in the US, because whenever he walked out of the theatre he was surrounded by love and that was of his fans; they truly loved his talent.

'Sammy was a very generous person and he spent money like water running from a tap. I was in awe of all the money he spent, but his attitude was, well, you can't take it with you and so he spent and spent. It was an amazing time, truly.

'Sammy also had parties in the theatre for the crew. I mean, he was that generous because for a lot of the stars they never bothered with us up there, you know, in the lights and sound – we were forgotten, but he was a superstar.' Did they ever hit the town after a show? 'Oh yes, I have partied with Sammy Davis Jr,' he laughed.

Linford now looked totally at home in the Val Parnell bar. 'Mr Lloyd Webber loves this theatre. Since he bought it he has spent millions on doing the place up and I am happy because she deserves it; it's our heritage.'

Linford had some favourite stars too. He described Harry Secombe as 'a brilliant person, always totally nuts and always smiling and laughing'. What a talent and great for the box office, too.

'Frankie Vaughan was a gentleman,' he went on. 'He was always dressed so smartly and all the ladies in the theatre had something of a crush on him, I think. But he was not big headed, you know what I mean? He just took it all in his stride and made people happy doing what he did best – entertaining.'

I discovered that not all the stars have been so well-mannered towards Linford. He is not too afraid to spill the beans. 'Tommy Steele is a professional man but can be a bit of a misery. But then, I suppose he is always smiling on stage so maybe when off, you know, he likes the down. For me, Charlie Drake, I don't know why – maybe it was because the show he was in was not going well – but he never seemed happy and so I gave him a wide berth. Not one to cross, really.'

Lindord told me how he had met all the major royals including Princess Margaret, Prince Charles and the late great Princess Diana. 'She was so beautiful and kind, a true lady. I was very upset when she passed away; many of us were, here at the theatre.'

Linford is now something of a celebrity himself at the theatre, with many people wanting to shake his hand and talk about the greats. While he is a naturally shy man, something tells me that he secretly enjoys his late burst of fame.

He finishes by telling me, 'I love this place and I don't plan to retire. I don't think they will allow it anyway, but you know, if I passed away here I would be happy because I have spent so many happy nights here. I could not have asked for a better life and showbiz has given me just that – a wonderful life.'

Hank Marvin
28 October 1941 – present

Hank Marvin is best known as the face and sound of the sixties group, the Shadows, and went on to have massive hits with tracks like 'Apache'. Hank came along to the studio to talk about his new album and soon the conversation turned to all things showbiz, including *Thunderbirds* and starring in panto at the London Palladium in 1964.

Hank is youthful-looking and great company; he drops showbiz names like gold. When you see just what he has achieved you are left slightly in awe, but I really wanted to know why and how he and the Shadows landed the Palladium panto.

'It's an odd one, that,' he said, 'because only a few years before we had been seen as this dangerous group with a lead singer who was corrupting the youth of the UK. Then suddenly were starring in a family friendly pantomime at the biggest theatre in the land, so yeah, an odd one.' *Aladdin* opened in late 1964 to a record-breaking box office and starred other showbiz legends such as Sir Cliff, Una Stubbs and the king of all clowns, Charlie Cairoli.

Hank continued, 'It was an amazing time and we did so well with the takings. I know the bosses were pleased and we enjoyed playing to a packed house nightly. I loved doing panto, to be honest, as it was good clean family fun. The upshot of it is that we were so successful they asked us back again two years later to reprise our success. It was *Cinderella* and another great time, because now we had got over our nerves. We also had a cast that included Terry Scott and Hugh Lloyd as the Ugly Sisters, Peter Gilmore as the prince and Jack Douglas as Baron Hardup, which created a wonderful atmosphere to work in every night. You can't believe your luck, really.'

Hank went on, 'Looking back, I think we realise how exciting it was to be at that theatre. We became regulars there, with TV shows and concerts, but it's only now, looking back, that it really sinks in. You remember what you did when you were young. I remember being excited to see my name outside the theatre and thinking what an achievement it was, but I see it all more clearly now.'

Hank also let slip something that I know will appeal to fans of the cult hit show *Thunderbirds*. He told me that the Shadows and Sir Cliff all appeared in the show and this was at the height of the success of the Lew Grade series. With a slightly glum face, he revealed, 'I don't have my doll. I wish I did, but I think when they had finished filming with them it was chucked in the bin. I know, tragic, and when you think now what they could be worth – but then again, hindsight is a great thing, don't you think?'

Frankie Howard
6 March 1917 – 20 April 1992

Frankie Howard, I have to confess, was not one of my favourites when I first met him simply because, at that time in the 1980s, all the stopping and starting in his routine really slowed it down for me. I even wondered why we were doing an interview at all, but he had a new show at the Garrick Theatre in London – a 'rebirth' – and while I was slightly concerned, I was equally intrigued.

Truthfully? He was a joy, a real gentleman, and we got on like a house on fire. Looking back at the interview now, I think I was looking at a man who was at peace with himself. He knew where he was and what he was doing and was very open in discussion.

As he poured the tea I remember him saying, 'Don't let anyone tell you comedy is an easy game. Oh no, honestly, it's tough, and then you have to bat off the competition like flies, dear, and I mean like flies. The thing with humour is it's in and out [of favour] and I have been both in and out, but there is no reason why it can't all come back. Look at me. Here I am again, back in the West End, but I have been on the other side where people have looked away when they have seen me approaching – I know what a cold shoulder looks like,' he laughed.

Francis Alick Howard was born on 6 March 1917 in a two-up, two-down terraced house in York, which spilled down to the River Ouse. His father was a sergeant in the Royal Artillery and his mother worked in a chocolate factory. So, although the Howard's were not especially 'well off', they were certainly not as poor as Frankie would allude to in later years. This was something he admitted to me in our interview. 'I was advised to play down my money and my connections, you know, because it would look better if it sounded like something out of *Oliver!* with the begging bowl, so I agreed to do it, but I did not agree with it. I was young and needed advice, really.'

Frankie's new show at the Garrick was billed as 'a comeback show' but to him he had never really been away. It was simply a case of moving in and out of vogue, and seeing him gear up for the show was an amazing experience. He was a real trouper and professional.

He spoke of his debt to another comedy hero, Eric Sykes. 'Eric knew what made me tick, so it all worked really well. The stuff he wrote was the kind of stuff that made us both laugh. He is a genius and I say that with love; he really is and he can do so many things. But I think, again, it's only by getting older and wiser that you can appreciate the breaks and the openings you had in your career, don't you?'

Frankie told me that he was totally happy with his first ever TV series, *The Howard Crowd*. He said, 'While I looked ill all the time on screen, the saving grace was having the glamorous Beverley Sisters on the show. They were wonderful and really helped me feel at ease because I was so nervous. As I told them, I am alone out there, dear, on that stage. Not three, just me,' he joked.

Frankie spoke of his big Palladium pantomime as Idle Jack in *Dick Whittington*, produced by Val Parnell. It also starred Richard Hearne, Sonnie Hale, Vanessa Lee and the great Warren Mitchell, who gained true stardom with 'Till Death Us Do Part'.

Frankie recalled, 'You know, the best bit about the show for me was the adlibbing. Mr Parnell was not keen on that, but I told him that I struggle to remember scripts and this was going over so well, why not just leave it in? Almost every day I was required to go and see him but in the end I think I just wore him out,' Frankie laughed.

'It was a big deal to get a panto like that at the Palladium, because it really was the main event. It's not like pantomime now, you see. We even had the famous Sky Rockets Orchestra. I mean, can you imagine that today, having that type of production?'

Frankie also revealed how the Palladium audiences really helped his nerves. 'I have always suffered with nerves, but after a few bad shows I would go back there (to the Palladium) and that helped no end, really, because you knew that a warm welcome waited.'

I sat through Frankie's new show and was won over. I still have the programme and was totally in awe of his talent and his quick-witted adlibs. There was very little in the way of the stop-start I used to fear.

It struck me that he was terribly insecure but, like so many, when they get out there on stage it all just happens, no problem at all. I came away thinking I had just witnessed a performance by a comedy great.

I met his good pal, actress June Whitefield, and she said something that put it into perspective. 'The thing with Frankie – he was one of the best, but I honestly believe if he had won the pools or the lottery he would have given it all up. I think there were times when he had had enough and he often said it.'

Robin Gibb
22 December 1949 – 20 May 2012

Bee Gees brother and undeniable superstar Robin Gibb was a singer-songwriter who shaped many lives with his inspiration and unforgettable songs.

Robin made one of his very last appearances at the London Palladium and he said this about the venue that meant so much to him, 'I did the *Coming Home* concert here because when you think of England you think of this place, don't you, certainly in terms of entertainment. I am honestly thrilled to be standing on that stage and doing what I do. We have done a few Royal Variety things, but I always thought the star of the show was the Palladium itself.'

Robin gave a moving performance leaving many of the audiences in tears and rightly so; we lost him shortly afterwards, far too early, due to illness.

As the great man said himself, 'I played the Palladium. How many can say that, eh?'

Charlie Watts
2 June 1941 – present

Charles Watts was born in London and joined one of the biggest bands in the world, the Rolling Stones. The group debuted in 1962 and enjoyed mega hits, such as 'I Can't Get No Satisfaction', 'As Tears Go By' and 'Start Me Up'. In recent years, Watts has gained fame as part of the swing group ABC&D of Boogie Woogie.

I was summoned to interview Charlie and his band mates ahead of their return to Hyde Park in 2013, which was a celebration of their famous 'free' Hyde Park concert in 1969. As cheerful Charlie pointed out, 'It does cost a bit more this time around.'

The brief was to speak only about the tour and new album and avoid boring him – tricky, when he must have received every question going about his career and the Rolling Stones.

I looked at the famous date of 22 January 1967, when the band appeared on *Sunday Night at the London Palladium*, and I figured this would be a slightly different route to his attention. Above all, I wanted to find out why the band had refused to appear on the famous revolve at the end of the show. The cast included Shani Wallis, Dave Allen and Ukrainian Cossacks.

Charlie remembers, 'I know, I was excited by it because I came from more of a showbiz side, to be honest, and I knew what a big deal it was, but honestly you have to remember this was the sixties and being 'cool' – well. The now-famous story about us not wanting to go on the famous revolve – I seem to recall it came from our manager, who thought if we refused we would get more exposure and be remembered, plus we had a new album and single out so the idea was quite valid.

'I actually felt sorry for the comic Dave Allen, who was the host of that show, because he tried his best with us but, you know, some thought it was old hat to be on the show – I loved it,' he smiled.

'Looking back,' Charlie added, 'it was great foresight as people do remember it. If we had done what everyone had wanted us to do, it would have been just another TV appearance, so yeah, we did right not to stand on that thing, really.'

Michael Crawford
19 January 1942 – present

Michael was born in Salisbury, Wiltshire, and he didn't hang around about chipping away into the industry. On leaving school he made his money by working on many different radio programs and children's movies. Some notable works from his youth are *Let's Make an Opera*, *Soap Box Derby* and *Come Blow Your Horn*. At the age of nineteen, he starred in the movie *The War Lover* with American actor Steve McQueen and perfected an American accent in a day in order to get a part in the movie. 'I was so determined to do it,' he told me.

In the middle of the eighties, Andrew Lloyd Webber had written a musical based on Gaston Leroux's

Phantom of the Opera. His then-wife, Sarah Brightman, was taking singing lessons from the same teacher as Michael. One day Andrew came to pick Sarah up after her lesson and he happened to hear Michael singing 'Care Selve' (from Handel's opera *Atalanta*). He was so impressed with what he heard that he cast Michael as the Phantom, the role which he has become most famous for.

As I sit down for an interview in the Val Parnell bar with Michael to discuss Phantom and many more aspects of his stellar career, he tells me, 'That story is true, yes, Andrew came in and heard me singing and then said to Sarah, "I think we have found our Phantom." Honestly, I was mortified as I really thought that, you know, this great composer had been subjected to hearing me sing and, well, the rest as they say is history.'

Michael is a fun guy, slightly shy, and looks decades younger than his age even though he tells me he has slowed down a bit since we last met. It can't be true, as he looks no different.

I was told by the PR of the show not to mention one of Michael's most famous TV hits, *Some Mothers Do 'Ave 'Em*, as (apparently) 'it's not relevant'. Really?

Michael starred as the accident-prone Frank Spencer in thirteen episodes of *Some Mothers Do 'Ave 'Em* and people loved him. It was a big hit. Frank Spencer returned to the TV screens the following two years with Christmas specials and another run of *Some Mothers* was shown in 1978. How could this not be relevant?

The sour faced PR woman sat guard during our interview until she felt the cold chill of 'you're not needed' from the both of us. She departed and our chat started to roll.

'I loved doing *Mothers*,' he told me. 'It was great fun and a lot of hard work but looking back, you know, it was ahead of its time and thankfully still gets repeated a lot, which is nice, because now I have grandchildren who can enjoy it. I am happy with it and yes, I still like the occasional look at it myself.'

While we sat in the lounge of the Palladium, Michael looked around at the many posters adorning the walls, which feature greats like Norman Wisdom and Grace Fields, and told me that he has the greatest admiration for 'variety turns', as he calls them, because they are so brave.

'As a child I listened a lot to the radio. We all did back then, but I always loved listening to the comedians as I always thought they were so brave, going out there. No scripts, just asking to be liked and to be funny. It's a skill, you know, and it's one I greatly admire.'

He added, 'When I was doing "Barnum" here we had an old variety turn, who was a huge help in getting me to learn how to interact with the audience. He showed me how to do the old stuff like a front cloth comedian. I was in awe of him, truly I was – he held no fear at all.'

Michael is another huge favourite of the royal family. He recalled one appearance at the London Palladium that left him with quite a funny feeling. 'Oh yes, it's great being on a Royal show but the nerves are sky high and for me, on that show, it was the worst. They asked me to close it – yes, close it – singing one number from *Jesus Christ Superstar*. It's a great honour, but terrifying, as every time someone came off it reminded me of the time I had left to go on,' he laughed.

The 1992 Royal Variety show was very special to Michael. The queen had requested that he topped the bill and appeared on the show. He smiled and said, 'I know how thrilling that is, but then, I don't suppose the queen suffers from stage fright, do you?'

That was Michael, great fun and totally at ease, which in turn made the interviewer (me) feel very comfortable. He went onto to say why he agreed to take the role of the Wizard in the *The Wizard of Oz* at the Palladium. 'Well, it's this place, of course, and the fact I loved it so much and really enjoy every comeback. I also don't think that my grandchildren have ever really seen this side of me. I had been "Poppa", who could be kind but was also a bit strict and serious, and this show was the best tonic ever because they loved the show and I loved the fact they were seeing me on the stage of the London Palladium.'

He was on the billing for the Royal Variety show that year as well and admitted he still got a bit excited and star-struck. He was joined by relatively new acts such as Adele, John Bishop and Susan Boyle and told me, 'I was in awe of Adele. I mean, they say talent is not what it was, but take a look at those three. I mean, it was amazing and of course they have come through in a short time, too.'

Michael teases that he may not be undertaking as many shows in the future. 'I like a challenge and all that, but I am not sure. Let's see what happens.' However, he did confide in me that any show that has the Palladium attached to it would be 'very hard to turn down'. So perhaps we do have something to look forward to.

Janet Jackson
16 May 1966 – present

Janet Jackson is an American recording artiste and actress. She is the youngest child of the Jackson family of musicians. She is best known for the hit singles 'Nasty', 'Rhythm Nation', 'That's the Way Love Goes', 'Together Again' and 'All For You'. Perhaps surprisingly, Jackson is ranked as one of the best-selling female artistes in the history of contemporary music.

Meeting Janet is always a thrill as she bursts with passion about her new projects. You get a genuine feeling that she truly loves to perform. When I asked her about appearing in the Royal Variety show, she beamed. 'It was Michael who told me, "Janet, you have to do it. It's for the queen and it's such a special occasion." Michael also told me of his love of the venue. We both had a copy of the classic Marvin Gaye album *Live at the London Palladium* and we played it all the time, so naturally, you know, Michael is a curious guy and begins to read up all about it. Plus we had friends like Diana (Ross) and other entertainers who had appeared there so he was kind of super excited and really happy that I had been asked.'

I asked Janet what she remembered in particular about appearing on the Royal show. 'Oh yes, lots of things, really, but my main memory of the show was the host, Sir John Mills, who had such a super English accent. I know many of the US stars were in awe of him because he spoke so beautifully; he was charming and very kind to me. I also remember meeting the Queen Mother, who was a lovely lady and still had a sparkle in her eyes. It was such a happy time for me.'

Max Bygraves
16 October 1922 – 31 August 2012

Max Bygraves is part of the fabric of the London Palladium; his good looks and easy going style wowed audiences for decade after decade at the theatre. Max himself was far more direct about his own success, telling me, 'It's down to being the everyman. You see, you make it look easy and then people think, oh, I can do that, but in reality they can't. That is what makes a star.'

By the mid-fifties Max was earning £1,000 a week, worth around £20,000 in today's money. His albums sold over 6.5 million copies, earning him some thirty-one gold discs; he loved to show them off, saying, 'See, people do buy my records.'

Max Bygraves also topped the bill at more Royal Variety Performances than any other artist, appearing in no fewer than seventeen shows. He was loved by the royal family such that the Queen Mother would request his presence every year. At one point she had to be asked, ever so nicely, to give other performers a chance by not asking for him.

Max also enjoyed the good life, buying the first of fifty-three Rolls-Royces with the registration MB 1. He liked to boast how he changed the car every year.

Max was a huge success on radio, too, with a hit in the 1950s radio comedy *Educating Archie* and his catchphrase, 'That's a good idea, son.' He also had a number of TV series such as *Singalongamax*, *Max Rolls On*, *Side by Side* and the game show *Family Fortunes*.

Max appeared in films, including *Charlie Moon*, *A Cry from the Streets* and *Spare the Rod*, and also starred in numerous pantomimes. Of his films, he told me, 'I did hope that one day I might just make it to Hollywood but it was never to be.'

I met Max on his last ever stint in the UK, when he was still drawing in huge crowds, but he admitted, 'We do afternoon shows now, as they lock the care homes up by six.' He was sharp, kind and very funny, plus he was exactly how you expected him to look off stage – great clothes and fresh-faced, even at that age.

I asked him about his memories of the Palladium and he recalled, 'I had some great times at the Palladium but I did not always agree with the boss, Val Parnell. You see, he has built a reputation of booking big US stars to lure in the crowds; a good idea, but then us Brits had to shore up the bill at very low rates.

'When Judy Garland first came over,' Max expanded, 'she was very nervous but also commanded a big fee, so Val stripped my fee from £100 to a mere £75 to help pay her. Now, we were a sell-out, but you know, that is how he did it and many were unhappy about that.'

Max had nothing but admiration for Judy, though, and told me she was a vastly underrated performer to begin with, as well as being gripped by insecurity. 'She was in the tops, really. She could do the lot and yet needed constant assurances that she was any good, which baffled us greatly because she had no idea just how good she was. She would insist, later in the run, that I join her or simply walk her on to the stage as she sometimes could not let go of the curtain in the wings. You would have to drag her on but then, once there in the glare of the Palladium spotlight, she changed – she got taller and more self-assured and commanded the stage. The audience did not want her to leave.'

Max told me that the season with Judy was a great boost. 'After that, I got the chance to appear on Broadway with her. Can you imagine that, so soon after the war?'

Max also went on to tell why the London Palladium was so appealing to an act. 'You have to remember that the company that ran the Palladium, Moss Empires, controlled the entertainment world, basically, and so if you were lucky enough to work with them then you were "in". They owned many theatres, from Scotland to London and all the big coastal towns for the much needed summer season; above all else, they could keep you in work for years if they liked you.'

Max spoke of the much-dreaded Moss Empire booker Cissie Williams. 'Oh, she was a one-off lady, really, but then again, she knew what she liked and every Monday night she would be at the Finsbury Park Empire, flask of tea and sandwiches in hand, scoring the acts and looking at what went well and what did not. So yeah, a tough lady in many respects but then it was her job, so you can't be too harsh about it, can you?'

After our interview I saw Max at work and he totally controlled the audience, telling wonderful stories and delivering gags galore, making everyone laugh and forget their troubles. He was a star and a professional and he left me with a great parting thought. 'You have to tell an audience when to laugh. No really, you need to signpost it for them and that has been the key to my success.'

Neil Sean, Live at the London Palladium (Finally)

It's almost the end of the book or, as I prefer to call it, 'bringing the curtain down'. It's funny when you look out at an empty theatre – many times, in my case, and with my act it's been like this when it's been open too – but I digress. All theatres are beautiful palaces of happiness and the Palladium is how I see it; we all go in to sit in the dark many times, surrounded by complete strangers with one wish in mind – to be taken away to a fantasy land of laughter and escape then come out smiling, hopefully having had an ice cream and some chocolate in the interval.

The Palladium has seen its fair share of bad shows, but no one goes into a show or indeed puts one on with the goal of making it bad – well, not unless you're Mel Brooks with the hit show *The Producers*.

My own dream to see my name at the Palladium came true in 2014. Yes, I had appeared there before but this time it was my production and act. Nervous? Not half. But then, I had been working towards this ever since mum and dad got me hooked on the Royal Variety shows on TV.

We decided to host an 'Audience with … ' style show, produced by Ann Montini and Mark Grant (I decided, finally, that I could not do it all). The date was set, thanks to the swift organization of Gareth Parnell, and we were off.

The first few months of the year were focussed on which star I would screen, the gossip I would and could reveal and, more importantly, how to get an audience. Now, this is the thing; because of the name of the Palladium we were able to sell out in record time, albeit with a sensibly priced ticket, and that was it. Now the nerves kicked in and I was left pondering, 'Can I actually do this?'

The date came around all too fast and suddenly we are there, arriving not in a swanky car but by the 94 bus; northerners never spend when they have bought a travel card.

After much flurry in setting up and checking props and so forth, the general manager uttered the immortal words, 'There is a mega queue outside. Can we open the doors?'

My tummy turns over and the reply is, 'Yes.'

Pretty soon, under mum's great direction and swift producing skills, we are off. It went better than I could have ever hoped for. A full house and hearing laughter at my gags – yes, real laughter – well, it was an amazing feeling.

Projected on the wall, directly looking at me, were the four people who shared the dream and would have been so happy to see that we, our family, had finally made it to the London Palladium.

So May, Phil, Con and Alan – this has been for you and I hope you enjoyed the show!

The curtain comes down and the lights go out.

Neil and Joan Rivers. She loved the Palladium so much. Our last chat together two weeks before she passed away was, as always, fun and gossipy – a true theatre legend.

Neil and Lionel Blair. 'It was and remains my favourite venue. I totally adored playing there and often go out of my way just to walk past it again.'

Neil with Jason Donovan. 'No one told me you don't arrive at the stage door on your push bike. They said, "No, you're the star – behave like one!" So I did.'

Neil with Michael Crawford. 'I used to stand outside in disguise, looking up at my name in lights outside the world famous London Palladium.'

Neil with Mickey Rooney. 'They said I was ill and cut short my stay, but truth is, I was a trail blazer. No one had actually done Hollywood variety before – I did, though.'

Neil with Ricci Martin. 'My dad, Dean, told me that he and Harry did not have the best first-time experience at the theatre, but they warmed to him in the end.'

Neil with Bill Kenwright. 'To see my name on a sign saying "Bill Kenwright presents Tommy Steele", well – you've made it, right? I knew it, and thankfully, so did my mum.'

Neil with Tony Bennett. 'I told them, I want to play the Palladium. People laughed, but here I am in my eighties, still playing this great venue.'va